GW01236964

Double Journey

A story of Christian Deliverance

Jack Butterfield

Prisoner-of-War of the Japanese in World War 2

Note for Librarians: a cataloguing record for this book that includes Dewey Decimal Classification and US Library of Congress numbers is available from the Library and Archives of Canada. The complete cataloguing record can be obtained from their online database at:
www.collectionscanada.ca/amicus/index-e.html
ISBN 1-4120-4495-2

Printed in Victoria, BC, Canada

Printed on paper with minimum 30% recycled fibre. Trafford's print shop runs on "green energy" from solar, wind and other environmentally-friendly power sources.

TRAFFORD
Offices in Canada, USA, Ireland and UK

This book was published *on-demand* in cooperation with Trafford Publishing. On-demand publishing is a unique process and service of making a book available for retail sale to the public taking advantage of on-demand manufacturing and Internet marketing. On-demand publishing includes promotions, retail sales, manufacturing, order fulfilment, accounting and collecting royalties on behalf of the author.

Book sales for North America and international:
Trafford Publishing, 6E–2333 Government St.,
Victoria, BC v8t 4p4 CANADA
phone 250 383 6864 (toll-free 1 888 232 4444)
fax 250 383 6804; email to orders@trafford.com

Book sales in Europe:
Trafford Publishing (uk) Ltd., Enterprise House, Wistaston Road Business Centre,
Wistaston Road, Crewe, Cheshire cw2 7rp UNITED KINGDOM
phone 01270 251 396 (local rate 0845 230 9601)
facsimile 01270 254 983; orders.uk@trafford.com
Order online at:
trafford.com/04-2303

10   9   8   7   6   5   4   3

CONTENTS

Foreword

By the Very Rev. Dr. Brandon D. Jackson LL.B., Dean of Lincoln
1989 - 1997

John Alfred Butterfield was brought up on a council estate in the West Riding of Yorkshire. He was called up in 1940 and for six years served in the Royal Army Medical Corps, three and a half years of which he spent as a Japanese Prisoner-of- War in Singapore and Thailand. That Jack (as he is generally known) survived was not a little due to the native cunning he had learned at his mother's knee and beyond, although he puts it all down to the grace and mercy of God which, of course, is also true.

Here is a man who to outward appearances is just another faithful and unremarkable member of his local church, an ordinary church in a run of the mill town just north of Bradford, West Yorkshire. He has been there all his life and graced most of the offices - choir, Parochial Church Council, Churchwarden and so on.

There have been many accounts written by many other P.O.W.s, most of which never got published. Why should this one be treated any differently? Because this is yet more proof that God does call and equip ordinary people to do extraordinary things extraordinarily well. The strong conviction of his calling coupled with his fierce modesty, honesty and the humility attaching to all he does, coupled with his expectancy that God can and will answer prayer, makes this story one that ought to be shared.

DOUBLE JOURNEY is a most moving account of a young man returning from World War 2 and re-discovering the love of a beautiful flame-headed Yorkshire girl. It is his account of his struggle to set up home and family with her in post-war Britain, racked by ration books and coupons, power cuts and low wages and all the hardships that characterized that decade. In trying to pick up where he left off is where we see the strength of character so vividly displayed, a strength that had been tested and proved through those painful years as prisoner-of-war. The growing discovery of both his and God's real identity is the pivot that swings this story into an epic of God's doing. His struggle with his watch-glass manufacturing business and his growing awareness of deep spiritual perception and consequent ministry are intertwined as naturally as they happened.

I felt very honoured and humbled when Jack asked me to write this foreword. Looking back on my years at Lincoln Cathedral, and reading this remarkable tale of God's power over Satan demonstrated again and again in the life and ministry of Jack Butterfield, I now find myself wishing I had asked him to visit us and give counsel and wisdom — and the way of deliverance — in the spiritual battle against evil.

The final chapter is a distillation of many profound truths learned through years of experience and all illustrative of those parts of Scripture that the rest of us ignore and are the poorer for it. For that alone, this book needs to be read by every minister and pastor of every church. It will throw light in dark places.

This book is well written by a man well skilled with his hands and wise towards God. It is a book of many virtues and not least tackles the questions that most of us avoid. Just how is divine power active in the world? Is not belief in such a power simply a retreat from science into magic — or is it the key that unlocks the mysteries of God's Universe?

Preface

It was as long ago as the 1980s that it was first suggested that I write this book. The person concerned was a dignitary of the Anglican Church in the Diocese of Bradford, West Yorkshire. He was a source of wisdom and guidance to me during a time when sinister, divisive forces were at work within the diocese. It is because I know he really meant what he said that I eventually set about the task of writing the book. It is his wish that he remain anonymous. Only after several years of revision and additions to the manuscript did I finally decide to seek publication.

"Double Journey" falls naturally into three parts. In the first section I give a brief account of happenings during my three and a half years as a Japanese Prisoner-of-War in Singapore and Thailand. I recount how, in retrospect, I could see how I had been protected in remarkable ways from what could have been certain death. I believe the reader may agree that the events I relate are too remarkable to have happened by mere chance.

The middle portion is concerned with a time of confusion and depression spanning many years. This had its beginnings in the fear and trauma experienced during those years of captivity. I relate how I sought help from these things, none having been received either from the medical profession or the local Anglican Church which I attended. I tell of how I was drawn into even more depression and torment when I accepted help from the wrong quarter, and how I subsequently came to experience the reality of many aspects of occultism. As I sought to see where my churchgoing fitted in, awful things began to happen to me. The story of how I was rescued from this is, I believe, an exciting one.

The final section tells of how I became spiritually equipped to deal with the forces of evil in the lives of others through a ministry of deliverance. This was recognised at Diocesan level in 1979 when I sought to become a Lay Reader in my parish church. Thereafter I describe some of the many cases of exorcism or deliverance in which I had the privilege to be involved over the next twenty years. Finally, I share with those engaged in this special ministry some insights gained during that time.

John A. Butterfield
September 2004

1

An unexpected welcome to Singapore

I lounged comfortably in a shady spot on the main deck of the old square-funnelled French vessel which lay stationary some miles outside Singapore.

Lifting my eyes I surveyed the archipelago of mini-islands that surrounded us. I took in the clear expanse of blue sea glistening brilliantly in the tropical morning sunlight, and was almost overcome by the beauty of the scene. It led me to reflect on the many other such surprises, some equally beautiful but different, experienced during the long sea voyage I had shared with the thousands of other men who made up our 18th Infantry Division. We had sailed from the Clyde some three months before and since then had enjoyed the privilege of visiting foreign parts at His Majesty's expense. We had left Bombay in good spirits on what was to be the last leg of our journey. Even the five-day wait off-shore before our departure had been tolerable. I had never lost interest in the constant activity at this great port. Countless multi-coloured small boats with their peculiar shapes and rigs had provided us with an ever-changing kaleidoscope of Oriental beauty.

As we zigzagged our slow way eastwards across the Indian Ocean with just one destroyer as escort I had become aware of a sombre, more serious mood developing among the men. The news of the attack on Pearl Harbour some weeks earlier and its implications for us had finally sunk in. We had realised the truth at last, that we were steaming towards the war zone - and the Japanese. The old French boat, the Felix Roussel, that relentlessly each day carried us nearer to our unknown destination, had begun to lose its original charm. Suddenly it had looked older and expendable. The drinking water had become contaminated and some of the food had rotted. To make matters even worse, an outbreak of 'flu had swept through the ship. By this time several more vessels had joined us, and it was with strangely mixed feelings of relief that we had seen, one morning, the coast of Java appear on the horizon. Yet our hopes of a landing there were soon to be dashed, as the ship suddenly changed direction. The captain had received orders to proceed to Singapore.

As I heard this news my mind went back sharply to a strange experience that had occurred soon after we set sail from the UK. At the beginning of our voyage our convoy had been steaming in a westerly direction out into the Atlantic, yet suddenly I had become aware, almost as if someone had told me, that our destination was to be Singapore. It seemed absurd at the time, but the experience had been so real that it had remained with me. As a normal twenty-three year old I had no knowledge or belief in anything outside my then exciting, down to earth, material existence. It was later that I came to recognise that I had received inner promptings even earlier in my life. Only later did I become aware of another dimension of consciousness and experience.

Our journey into Singapore had involved travelling through a narrow strait that runs between the island of Bangka and Sumatra. Two other ships had accompanied us. I shall always remember that part of our journey. The strait, about fifty miles long, was so narrow in parts that one could see clearly the mangrove swamps on either side, reaching out far into the water. We had steamed about half way through it when a number of Japanese aircraft came into view. The alarms were sounded, but almost before we could get below decks the planes had let loose a string of bombs. Fortunately they missed us. The planes obviously had been on their way to bomb targets in Java, and had continued on to their destination. However, we had then realised that there was now no chance of our being able to sneak into Singapore unnoticed. At daybreak next day we saw that one of the two ships that had been with us had disappeared. It had been the smaller and faster of the two, and no doubt had reached port before dawn. We had pressed on at maximum speed and by 10.00 a.m. were just a few miles from the docks. There we had stopped in order to take a pilot on board, who would guide us through the tricky traffic lanes outside Singapore.

As I relaxed in comfort on the ship's main deck, preoccupied by the beauty of my surroundings, I had forgotten the incident of the previous day. For some minutes I had relived only the pleasant. exciting experiences of our long sea cruise, which had been punctuated by a short stay in Cape Town and several weeks in India. My morale was high, and I recall no feelings of fear or any apprehension about the future.

Suddenly I was aroused from my reverie by a commotion among the men nearby. Two of my friends, who had been lying next to me, were suddenly on their feet. They were staring into the sky. Twenty-five Japanese dive-bombers appeared to be heading in our direction at a height of about 2000 feet. The alarm bells sounded, and everyone rushed for the stairways. I found myself at the back of the queue, and was still on deck when the 'all clear' sounded. The planes appeared to have passed on. Actually they had just flown into the sun, and a moment later they peeled off to attack us. Then the alarm sounded again, and there was chaos on the stairways.

That first surprise dive had been successful. I am still unsure of where we were hit, or if it was just a very near miss. I remember seeking my quarters, which were immediately below the main deck, and having to splash my way through water in dark, long corridors until I at last found them. All the lights had gone out. I found that most of my small unit (there were about thirty of us) had arrived before me. Most were sitting silently. The noise above us was deafening. Fortunately for us, travelling on our ship with us was a company of Northumberland Fusiliers, a machine-gun unit. Guns had been erected on the upper deck, and there was one larger gun in the centre of them. Men with ordinary rifles had been allocated to the main deck. There were no sandbags, nothing to protect them from shrapnel should bombs explode in the water. There is absolutely no doubt in my mind that but for the presence and bravery of that machine-gun unit the Felix Roussel would have been lost, along with the lives of many men.

Some fifteen minutes into the battle a call was made to us to mount a stretcher party to bring a dead gunner down from the upper deck. Our unit was a specialist medical section qualified to deal with water supplies and hygiene under tropical battle conditions, but we were also trained as medical orderlies. The response for four volunteers revealed the true mettle of some of those who, whilst in training back in England, had been derisory of the sort of work we were being trained to do. 'Why don't they give us some guns, so that we can do a man's job!', was the sort of thing they used to say. Now, at last, they had a perfect opportunity to demonstrate how brave they were! However, instead of jumping immediately to his feet, the chief advocate of this great doctrine protested that he had just recovered from 'flu and was not at all well! The fact was that most of us had suffered in exactly the same way. The first volunteer was my close pal Dick, who was only half the size of our unfit friend! Whilst in England, he also had been at the receiving end of mockery and scorn because he had spent most of his spare time making models of sanitation equipment. Our Commanding Officer used them in demonstrations to other units. Dick was a quiet chap, brilliant with his hands. Now he stood up and shouted, "Come on lads, we might as well die doing something as stay down here doing nothing!". Two other friends and myself followed him on deck. A terrible sight confronted us. Half a mile away, and broadside on, was the ship that had accompanied us, the Empress of Asia. It was on fire from end to end, and there were hundreds of men swimming in the sea. Its three decks still boasted the white paint that had emphasised its handsome lines in its peacetime role as a cruise liner. The planes now concentrated all their attention on the Felix Roussel. The four of us made our way as quickly as possible to the upper deck, but we had to take shelter at least once as planes dive-bombed and sprayed us with machine-gun fire. As they did so the noise was horrendous, as all our guns opened up on them. We finally got the body onto a stretcher, but we had to lie down again as bullets rattled past us only feet away.

4

Unfortunately the soldier manning the large gun was hit across the knees. He had to be dragged away, much against his will, continuing to curse and shout at his attackers.

We managed to get below again safely. We soon all realised how vulnerable our position was, situated as we were right under the main deck. A direct hit above us would blow us all to pieces. Each time we heard the guns open up we realised it could be the end for us. In fact we did have a very narrow escape when a bomb exploded in the water nearby and shattered the porthole glass in our compartment. Those glasses are several inches thick. After the battle we discovered that the bomb had passed straight through a lifeboat which had hung at that point. The hole was only a yard from the ship's side!

Suddenly we realised that the ship was moving! Somehow the pilot had been taken on board. The battle continued to rage for some time, then suddenly ended. We eventually reached the dock, and slowly inched into our berth. The dockside was completely deserted, and we had to tie up the ship ourselves.

We concluded later that the 'Japs' had either run out of fuel or ammunition. After one and half hours they had turned and left for home. They had lost five planes to our guns. Our casualties were five dead and twenty-five injured. I was told that of the two thousand men on the Empress of Asia two hundred had been either killed or drowned.

We heard that our ship left Singapore that night with civilians on board. The date was Friday, 5th February, 1942.

2

Countdown to captivity

We had been on the island over three days before the powers-that-be decided what to do with us. During our period in the U.K. our specialist section had been attached to Royal Army Medical Corps Field Ambulance units and with them had been trained for battle conditions in the Western Desert. Now we were out on a limb with no direct link with Command. We had moved twice during those first three days. On both occasions we had moved into bombed-out houses in an area between the city and the front line. The Japanese had already gained a foothold on the island and were advancing southwards. Our Section Commanding Officer, a young Scottish doctor who held the rank of major, finally decided to go back to the city and try to locate Command Headquarters. He eventually did so, and returned with orders to abandon our stores and to move into the city's Municipal Building.

At this point my friend Dick again exercised his initiative, something for which I had much cause to be grateful later. During our move into town he slipped away unnoticed and succeeded in locating the main Post Office building. He paid for telegrams to be sent to both our families, although he was warned that they may never get away. Years later, on our return home, we were to learn that the one sent to my own parents had indeed got through. It had read simply: "Safe and well." The news had been passed to Dick's family, and was the last anyone heard of us for three and a half years.

A somewhat macabre job had been allocated to our unit. Japanese bombers had for some time subjected the city to repeated "blanket bombing" attacks, and civilian casualties had been very high. In the tropical heat the dead bodies, many buried among the debris of fallen buildings, presented a serious health hazard. I can only assume that it was thought in high places that our specialist training in England had equipped us ideally to deal with this sort of problem! It was decided that some of us would take on the job of locating bodies and then loading them onto trucks. Others would travel with these to sites outside the city and there undertake their burial in mass graves. I was allocated to one of these latter parties.

The work lasted only one day. That was not because we had completed it - in fact, we had only just started. Nevertheless, the events of that day are indelibly engraved on my memory. The problem was that the Japanese troops were by this time (it was Friday, 13th February) within shelling distance of the city suburbs. On the outward journey from the bombed site six of us sat at the rear of a tipper wagon, our backs pressed hard against the tail-gate. Our grisly load of some twenty corpses was covered with tarpaulins. I still remember vividly the shattered limbs and long black tresses of women's hair that protruded in our direction from beneath the inadequate coverings. Although we covered our faces with handkerchiefs and smoked numerous cigarettes, the stench of decaying bodies still remained unbearable.

I was never told the name of the hospital which was our eventual destination. I estimated that we had travelled about three miles. On a hilly slope below the building was a large, newly excavated area about two hundred feet long and about twenty feet wide. We all jumped out of the wagon long before it stopped in order to escape the awful smell - if only temporarily. The hole was some six feet deep and had been only roughly dug out. The drop into it was not steep, and the tipper was reversed carefully until it overhung the edge. In the same way as it would normally have discharged a load of gravel, it slowly disgorged its dead human cargo. A few at a time the corpses slithered to the ground, leaving in front of us a jumbled human mass. Unmarked, some bodies looked like people who were just asleep. No doubt they had been killed by blast. The body of a heavily pregnant Malay girl, glassy-eyed and grotesquely folded, lay before us, her beautiful, lithe form and once-precious burden twisted in the rigidity of death. Wedged tightly between two bearded men was a baby, robbed of life after only a few months. Lying obscenely close to us was the almost naked body of an older Malay woman who had been stripped of her clothes by the intense blast of an explosion. Among other mutilated bodies we found that of a British soldier, his pipe stuck jauntily into the breast pocket of his tunic, ready to hand for his next fill of tobacco. We managed to find his pay book, and we handed it in later.

I remember that some of my friends were violently sick as we set about the task of covering the bodies with earth excavated from the site As I recall, I was emotionally quite unaffected, perhaps my mind and feelings had shut off from what was really happening. Sometimes today I feel guilty as I remember that occasion and other times when I have reacted in that seemingly unfeeling and heartless way to the death of strangers. Yet I console myself that when people seek to share personal experiences with me I have always, from deep inside been able "to rejoice with those who rejoice, and weep with those who weep" to use a Biblical phrase. The grief and damaging experiences of suffering and death do not rub off onto me. I am glad of this because as a consequence I am better able to help them. Of course, it is not quite so easy when problems lie nearer home.

Barely had we finished the job when, suddenly, the scream of shells overhead made us seek cover. It was soon evident that our road back to the city was the main target. As we found out later, the enemy was trying to pinpoint an important cross-roads a mile or two down the road. We took shelter inside the hospital for a while. I remember a ward sister who, quite unperturbed, made us all a welcome cup of tea.

After about thirty minutes there was a lull in the shelling. Not all our men were keen to make a run for it, but one of our drivers, who had brought extra men from town in a large, powerful American saloon, was eager to be off. He invited some of us to join him, and with some trepidation I and two other friends accepted the offer.

I shall never forget the high-speed drive back into the city.

8

Fortunately from the driver's point of view the road was almost dead straight, and he drove at maximum speed. Everywhere was completely deserted. Lining the road on either side were countless small shops. The multi-coloured Chinese business signs that hung out over the road flew by like so many flags waving in a great parade. Suddenly the shelling started up again, and there was an explosion a few hundred yards ahead. As our car screeched to a standstill we threw ourselves into the anti-malaria drains that flanked the road. These were fairly deep, open concrete drains designed to carry away quickly large volumes of rainwater. The shelling continued for about ten minutes. As soon as it stopped we tore off at speed and made it back safely to the Municipal Building. There we waited anxiously for the rest of our friends. They would be in the tipper wagon in which I had travelled to the hospital earlier in the day. About forty-five minutes passed, by which time we were getting really worried, when they arrived, all badly shaken. I remember Dick's face was ashen! They had been pinned down at the cross-roads for over half an hour, and several shells had landed much too close for comfort!

We spent all next day trying to dig a well in the grounds of the Municipal Building. The Japs had cut off the water supply. The day after that, Sunday, was the day we were told that General Percival, commander of the Allies, had surrendered to the High Command of the Nippon Imperial Army. Their troops were to occupy the city the next morning, Monday, 15th February, 1942, ten days after our arrival at Singapore.

On that our last afternoon of freedom Dick and I strolled across the cricket field which, like a little piece of England, separated the Municipal Building from the sea. Nearby lay the wreckage of a Jap fighter aircraft, its aluminium fuselage torn wide open. It was with mixed feelings that we saw, printed on the metal inside, the name of a British firm with its address, "Birmingham, England".

3

Out of the frying pan . . .

From an upstairs veranda Dick and I looked down on the truckloads of Japanese troops as they entered the city. I remember the look on their faces as they stared up at the imposing buildings, a look that seemed to combine childish wonder with a sense of pride in what they had achieved.

Within a few days we were told to make our way to Changi, in the north-east corner of the island. Here our captors were to establish the POW. camp in which they would contain the many thousands of Allied troops captured at the fall of Singapore. At first our unit remained together - minus its commanding officer - and we were allocated some wooden huts near Changi village. Gradually news trickled through of atrocities committed by the Japanese during and after the fall of city. I prefer not to relate all the sickening stories that reached us. I will recount just two incidents that I know to be true and which affected me personally. The first is concerned with John and Bob, who had been called up with me in March, 1940. They were medical orderlies in the R.A.M.C. Field Ambulance to which my own unit was at first attached. It was said that they were conscientious objectors who had nevertheless been prepared to serve in the Medical Corps. They were two super guys, who really seemed to enjoy the square-bashing we were all put through as raw conscripts. I shared a long, large barrack room with them and with upwards of another fifty men. Apparently they were Christians, and certainly were not ashamed of the fact. Each day, just before lights out, they would kneel together at the foot of their beds and say prayers. As I recall, no-one ever mocked them. Although I myself had been a church-goer right up to the day of my call-up, I remember thinking that there was something different about them. Perhaps at that time I thought they were just very religious.

During the battle for Singapore John and Bob were posted to Alexandra Hospital, the scene of one of the advancing army's worst atrocities. The Japanese troops completely overran the building, killing everyone in their path, even the surgeons and doctors and patients on the operating tables. I later met a survivor who had secreted himself in the underdrawing of the building. He told me how the Japanese soldiers had tied up the medical orderlies and had later bayoneted them to death in cold blood. In volunteering to serve in the Medical Corps my two friends had known, like all of us, that they may have to make the ultimate sacrifice for their country. I just found it difficult to understand why this had actually happened to two Christian young men.

We had been at Changi only a few days when the other incident took place. Apparently the new Japanese administration had advertised the fact that special jobs would be given to civilians who had held positions of responsibility under British rule. I am not absolutely certain of how many people responded. I think it was about a hundred and eighty, probably all male. Half this number were taken to a deserted beach near Changi and machine-gunned down. The remainder were brought there next day. Each person was tied to a dead body and together they were all taken by boat out to sea and dumped overboard. Amazingly two or three men had escaped fatal injury on the first day. Bullets had missed their vital organs. They managed to crawl inland towards the camp and our men took them to our so-called hospital area. Next day the Japs saw that some bodies were missing, and searched the hospital units for these men. I know that at least one escaped detection; he was an Anglo-Chinese who was eventually attached to our unit. Throughout his time as a prisoner-of-war his friends made sure that he always wore some sort of vest in order to conceal his scars. I am certain that an effect of these and other atrocities was to produce in us a degree of repressed apprehension and fear that remained with us throughout our captivity.

By the end of six weeks our store of rations had almost gone. Supplies of rice had not yet come through, and symptoms of vitamin deficiency diseases began to appear. I developed severe pellagra due to deficiency of vitamin B2. Fortunately for us, a Red Cross ship carrying vitamin supplies was allowed by the Japanese to enter Singapore. I believe it was the only such ship they ever allowed in. I received a ration of hydrolysed yeast extract over a period of three days and my symptoms vanished. I had been covered with ringworm from head to foot, and my mouth, throat and all mucous membrane areas had been terribly inflamed. Unfortunately, I discovered later that permanent damage had been done to nerve tissue.

The huts in which we lived were spread around what had once been an orchard. Within a day we stripped the trees of any bananas, prickly pears or other fruit that remained. There were several coconut palms around, all with nuts in profusion, but climbing them presented too great a challenge to any of us. Every so often though, usually at night, a squall would blow up and then, suddenly, thump! A coconut had fallen! Simultaneously a dozen pairs of feet would streak in the direction of the sound. Just once I was fortunate enough to share the succulent, still soft, white lining of the coconut that fell near our own hut. We were virtually starving at the time, and it tasted like nectar!

I have distinct memories of those weeks during which hunger never left us. A thing that surprised me was that the hunger pangs were experienced in my throat and not in my stomach. At one point some of us tried eating grass, but were violently sick. Eventually supplies of rice did come through, with daily quantities of vegetables such as sweet potatoes, green papayas and the like, but we had no meat or fat. Most mornings we had to work. One job was to bring into the camp large sacks of rice and then distribute them to different units. This we did using trailers from old lorries; it took six of us to push them, especially on any sort of incline. Gradually we settled down into a routine. Dick managed to make a small wood turning lathe from an old bicycle hub, and I designed an efficient fly-trap to use in the latrines - it became known as "The Butterfield Flytrap". Fame indeed! For those who wished to improve their education, "Changi University" was formed. Courses were arranged in various subjects, ranging from the sciences and languages to psychology and art. There was a wealth of qualified people amongst us to run these courses. They were destined to last only a limited time, however, as the Japanese soon began to move their prisoners out of the island. I attended a few sessions in Japanese and Russian. They were held in the afternoons when work for the day was complete. Morale was reasonably good, and the lads in our unit were quite content. We had been able to remain together, and friendship amongst us was real. That is why what happened to me next was so illogical and inexplicable.

One morning, whilst on parade, our staff-sergeant announced that he needed two volunteers to work in Singapore city. Apparently two medical orderlies were needed there. The camps were situated some miles away at the other side of the island. Our captors were using our troops as labourers to clear away the huge quantity of rubble created by the heavy bombing of the city. The handcarts which the Japanese had used for transporting their supplies down Malaya during the fighting were now being stacked with much heavier loads, and already this very hard work was taking its toll among our men. Working from dawn to dusk, and living on a diet lacking essential vitamins, they had soon developed scrotal eczema and ringworm. Dysentery had broken out and had begun to spread rapidly. I had heard about the camps in the city that housed these troops - a series of bamboo huts each of which held about a hundred men. It was for these camps that the two volunteers were needed.

For a full minute following the staff-sergeant's announcement nobody spoke. Then I felt a quite irresistible compulsion to raise my hand. I remember now that there was no logic behind this. There was no promise of more food or better conditions that might have persuaded me to go. I just felt my hand being raised as if my will were no longer my own. Then another hand went up, at the end of the rank. It was that of an Anglo-Indian medical orderly who had been attached to our unit after our capture. I did not know him.

Dick and my other friends were certain that I had taken leave of my senses. They were genuinely upset at the prospect of losing me. Anyway, they said, nobody ever volunteered for anything - that was an unwritten law. Yet nothing would persuade me to change my mind. It was some two years later that I received what I believe was the explanation for this strange behaviour. Next day I was despatched by truck, complete with kitbag and other possessions, to Havelock Road Camp in Singapore city. On arrival I discovered that there was not one square inch of space available for me. I could find nowhere to pitch my kit or to sleep. It was several days before I did in fact obtain some space. I was just surplus to requirements; the Japs did not really want me there. My presence was simply a token gesture made by them in response to pleas for medical aid. I had nothing to work with, and after a while my captors decided I would be of more use working outside the camp clearing the anti-malaria drains. I then had to operate as medical orderly after the evening meal of rice and weak stew. I soon used up my own small stock of ointments on my friends. Their thighs and scrotum had become red raw - the result of sweating continuously throughout their long, hot working day. Then the Jap lance-corporal under whom I worked issued me with a quantity of calamine lotion and some mysterious brown tablets. I never discovered what these were made of, but was told they would relieve diarrhoea. Later on in the evenings my Jap friend would engage me in long conversations about the war. He took great delight in showing me detailed plans for the invasion of Australia - published in an inch thick paper-back!

One morning I awoke with a raging temperature. It was quickly evident that I had got Dengue Fever, an unpleasant, debilitating disease that lasts about ten days. I was sent back to Havelock road camp and consigned to the "Hospital Hut". I had known the lieutenant medical officer in charge when in England. He was in the Field Ambulance unit to which I had been attached. I remembered him particularly because I had repaired his valuable, gold automatic winding watch.

After a pretty horrible ten days during which I had no desire to eat, I began to get better. I would be expected to resume work within days. Then, out of the blue, my lieutenant friend said to me: "Would you like to go back to Changi? If not, you'll be put on a ship shortly and sent to Burma. The Japs are building a railway from Thailand, and are working from both ends. The other bad news is that we are sinking our own chaps en route"! It took me no time at all to make up my mind. The next day I was sent back to Changi - ostensibly a dysentery patient.

The section of the P.O.W. camp reserved for the very ill, known as the "Hospital Area", was located some distance from Changi village where my unit had been sited originally. Dysentery had reached epidemic proportions. By now there were some three thousand patients, and there was no supply of drugs with which to treat the disease effectively.

Having arrived there with the dysentery patients from Havelock Road camp, I somehow had to get back to my unit near the village, now situated in what was called "Southern Area". The various areas were separated by rolls of barbed wire. Eventually I managed to obtain an official pass and fled post-haste to rejoin my pals. To my dismay, the unit was gone. After many enquiries I found that it had been attached to a Royal Signals company. I asked about my close friends who were not there. Particularly I wanted to know about Fred Tomlinson. Fred and I had been very close; in England we had spent all our off-duty time together, and had both been promoted to lance-corporal. I was told that he had been sent to Thailand on a working party a short time earlier, and had been made up to sergeant. It was the intention that I go with him, but in my absence they had sent Syd Dyson, a fellow-Yorkshireman from my home town. He also had received promotion. I remember my disappointment as I heard this news.

Three of my other pals, Dalton, Harrison and Smith, had left on the same party. Only a handful of us, including Dick, now remained in Singapore. Gradually I settled down again, and was even able to repair watches in my spare time, using the few tools and spares I had managed to hang on to. Because the camp guards, who were Koreans, let me repair their own watches I was given official permission to keep my tools. This was shown on a large printed label which I stuck on my repair box. I always received token payment for my work, and I was able to use this money later to buy any available food for myself and friends.

Several months went by. Although we were moved to another area, the remnant of our unit remained together, and the rest of the medics from the Field Ambulances were with us. Life had become boring and the food was terrible. Nothing, we thought, absolutely nothing could be worse than this!

One day it was announced that a party of one hundred medical orderlies and twenty-five medical officers was needed to go to Thailand. I met together with my pals and we decided to volunteer. The idea was that we should work together in groups, one doctor with four orderlies. It sounded slightly promising. After all, we had already decided that nothing could be worse than staying put! Later, and many times over, we came to know how wrong such assumptions could be.

We left Singapore in February, 1943. The train journey northwards was very unpleasant; it was boiling hot by day and very cold at night. We had been packed into steel, enclosed wagons normally used for transporting coal, and were soon black all over! We stopped overnight at Kuala Lumpur, where we slept on the station platforms. Next morning I sneaked over to a news kiosk where I found on sale a Japanese textbook printed in English. I bought a copy with some of the cash I had received from my watch repair work.

Our rail journey ended at a place called Bampong, just inside Thailand. It was a transit camp, and conditions there were terrible. Hundreds of our comrades had been brought down from the jungle labour camps dotted along the route of the railroad now under construction between Thailand and Burma. In that terrible, infected jungle these men had contracted cholera, dysentery, malaria, tropical ulcer and beri-beri (to name just the main diseases) and many of their friends had died. We soon wished from the bottom of our hearts that we had never volunteered to leave Singapore!

4

The Thailand – Burma Railway

We remained at Bampong just one week. During that time our twenty-five medical officers were forced to sit a written examination to prove their competence as doctors. This was just part of an attempt to demoralise us, and the idea did not work. The morale of the officers was high, and they were just amused at what they considered to be our captors' childish plan. The officers were also subjected to anti-British propaganda lectures. They were told:

"When you built the British Empire you used thousands of slaves from the East. When you built the Panama Canal countless lives were lost. Now it is your turn to suffer."

Late one afternoon we were told to be ready to move within the hour. All one hundred and twenty-five of us were ordered to climb onto about a dozen steel wagons that were already loaded with railway sleepers. After much hissing and spluttering the train finally moved off. Until it gathered speed most of us had to defend ourselves against showers of sparks that were being belched out of the engine's funnel. It appeared that they were using wood for fuel!

We had been travelling for some time through semi-jungle country when the railway line drew near to the river. What we then saw immediately ahead terrified us. There was a sheer drop of about a hundred feet at this point, and a two-tier bridge, probably two hundred feet long, had been built against the cliff. It was a complex mass of beams and tree-trunks, held together by joints and nails only. Slowly our train edged forward at about two miles per hour. Much creaking and grinding went on as we steadily inched our way across. Our twelve wagons were grossly over-loaded with sleepers, and we were perched on top of them. To our intense relief we got across safely, and the train stopped at a halt there. I believe this place, a P.O.W. labour camp, was called Wampo. We were met by a few English P.O.Ws who were staring at us aghast. "Yours is the first train ever to cross that bridge!", they shouted, dumbfounded. When we made the return journey over a year later two thirds of the bridge had been shored up with solid concrete.

Darkness had fallen by the time we reached the railhead. Under the glare of powerful lights much activity was taking place. We never got close enough to see exactly what was going on. The Japanese, their loud, harsh staccato voices competing with the noise of petrol-powered electricity generators, were obviously giving orders to men working on the line. The clang of metal on metal could be heard as rails were being laid and pinned to the sleepers.

Our party was moved away quickly to a spot where a number of covered lorries awaited us. We were bundled into these and immediately set off along a rough track that had been cut out of the jungle. It turned out that we were near the river at this point. Although the ground was fairly flat it was extremely uneven, and without warning the wagon I was in lurched to one side at a frightening angle. I lost my balance and was thrown to the floor. The Japanese driver continued on, quite unaware of the plight of some of his passengers. I and others found ourselves being trampled on, and at one point I was unable to breathe, and nearly passed out. We were soon rescued; nevertheless I still count that experience as one of the most frightening and traumatic of my life.

After about ten minutes the trucks came to a halt in some sort of clearing. We were told to lay out our groundsheets and get some sleep. There was a horrible smell around the place and one humorist amongst us said: "It's the smell of the jungle, chaps, it's the smell of the jungle!". Next morning we discovered the reality - we had been lying on ground that was well-manured with Tamil excrement. It seemed that the Tamils refused to dig communal latrines and preferred to use wide open spaces. It had something to do with their religion, apparently. Unfortunately it was a wonderful way of spreading fly-borne diseases.

After we had eaten our morning ration of rice we were moved to a spot near the river. There we were sprayed with some chlorine-smelling substance which was supposed to disinfect us. We were then put on board fairly small boats powered by outboard motors. It was at this point that our party was broken up into smaller groups of about ten. Dick was not in my group. We called these boats "pom-poms", after the noise they made as they chugged up and down the River Kwai. We had a doctor amongst our number called Major Roberts. Ever since our departure from Singapore he had been concerned to remain alongside me because by then I had acquired a smattering of Japanese. I did not quite understand at the time what advantage he thought that would give him. I still had the text-book purchased at Kuala Lumpur, and later this enabled me to make great progress in learning the language.

As we set off upstream early that sunny May morning I soon found myself entranced by the scenery on either side of the river. Monkeys or some related species swung with tremendous agility between the upper branches of the lofty, giant bamboo clumps that overhung the dark mass of jungle thicket right up to the water's edge. This idyllic scenery continued unbroken as we chugged upstream for over two hours. Then our boat pulled over towards the right bank to a spot where there was a break in the trees. We made a landing there.

The pleasure of that river journey had left us within minutes of stepping ashore. It was as if we had been the victims of a huge confidence trick. We seemed to have stepped out of light into darkness. Only a hundred yards or so from the bank were two large bamboo huts. As we moved across the smelly, boggy ground towards them the Jap in charge of us told us to go straight on. However, we were determined to look in, and did so. What we saw horrified us. Some two hundred prisoners, their bodies almost reduced to skeletons by dysentery or cholera, lay there apparently unattended. I believe that they had been deliberately put there in isolation and left to die. With shouts of "Speedo!, Speedo!", a sound that was to ring continually in our ears until the railway was completed, our Jap guide forced us to follow him. He said his name was Maki-san, and that we did not have far to go. Our journey was uphill, on a winding track that led to the railway line. All of us were carrying our kit-bags, many of them quite heavy. Eventually our burdens became just too much for us to manage up the long, steep, muddy path that lay before us. Along with some of the others, I began to discard things like books and other heavy items. We had walked seven kilometres by the time we reached our destination - a few small huts at the side of the railway line. The next day we met the Japanese major in charge of the whole party. His name was Dr. Matsumoto, and he seemed a benign enough fellow. He said that he had been an obstetrician in civil life. He told us we were to be split up again, and sent to join different working camps on the line. I was in a group of three. My companions were Dr. Roberts and a private soldier who had joined our unit just before we left the U.K. His name was Clive, and he was about nine years my senior. We left next day with a Jap soldier as guide, and had to walk several kilometres up the partly made rail-track until we reached a riverside camp called Hintock.

By this time the monsoon rains were well and truly with us. At the camp we worked under a Japanese soldier called Morohoshi. He was a "Joto-hei" - a first class private soldier. In the Japanese army there were three grades of private! Morohoshi was a medical orderly. We camped in a tent with him near the main hut occupied by the Jap engineers. He was quite decent to us and was very keen to learn English, of which he knew just a little. Occasionally in the evenings in the light of a crude lamp (made from a bit of wick in a small bottle of vegetable oil) he would try to improve my Japanese, and I his English. It was during this time that I got my pronunciation right. Not too long afterwards I began to think in the language.

An amusing incident occurred one evening. Our Nippon friend was sitting on an improvised stool made by us from the ever-ubiquitous bamboo. We had done this by driving into the ground two stakes a foot apart, with another two opposite them and about a yard away. We tied another bamboo across each of the tops, making two goal-post shapes. Then we put half a dozen four foot long bamboo rods across the "goal-posts" making a sort of bench. These were tied on with rattan, a strong fibre obtained from a climbing palm, which was used in making all the bamboo buildings. As the days went on, the rattan started to work loose. On the night in question Morohoshi found himself perching on just two remaining bamboo rods. With a grin spreading all over his face he announced: "Here I sit, like monkey!" The three of us who were watching just burst out laughing - not at Morohoshi's remark, but at the fact that he looked exactly like a monkey, features and all!

Shortly afterwards I remember the rain starting to come down in torrents. The next day the river rose about nine feet. The Japs had sited their cookhouse not far from the water's edge, and before evening they had re-sited it well above maximum water level. The river rushed down what was really a giant gully. It wound its way through the only gap in the mountains that led eastwards to the sea. This gully, with its steep, scarred sides had been carved out of the earth during thousands of years of monsoon rains. The downpour continued unabated for days. It made walking over the muddy ground more difficult, and produced a mist that hung everywhere below the impenetrable foliage of the seemingly endless bamboo forest.

One day I visited the isolation area set apart for British cholera victims. Not much was being done for these men; indeed, all that could be done in those terrible conditions was to give them as much boiled water as possible in order to fight dehydration. There was no equipment to provide a simple normal saline drip, which would have helped combat the excruciating cramps. Of the dozen or so men I met there, two stand out clearly in my memory. One, a tall Scotsman of fairly powerful physique was cursing God and Jesus as he writhed with pain. The other was a small man, an officer, who quietly bore his pain and said to me: "I intend to get better and get home to my wife and kids." He said it with a determination of spirit I clearly remember. The Scotsman died a few hours later; the officer stuck it out and recovered. Whether he ever made it back home I do not know. I am certain that his will to cling on to life had borne fruit, and had been a factor in his recovery. I came to see later that losing one's will to live can have the opposite effect.

Most of our time at Hintock was spent in supervising the burial of Tamil labourers who had died from cholera, dysentery or malaria. We liaised with the "head-men" in charge of their work-force. There was no hut within the camp set apart for use as a hospital. The Japanese were ruthless in their determination to complete the railway quickly. They would line up the Tamil workers at first light and select from them every person who could walk - even if only just - and send them off to work on the line. Women too were included. Their job was to complete the railway embankments by breaking up stones and tipping them between and at the side of the rails. This involved ceaseless trips throughout the day during which their meagre loads were carried on their heads in coracle-shaped wicker baskets. Those who were deemed unfit for work usually did not survive long. Those suffering from cholera were isolated in a clearing, well outside the camp area. They lay under small ridge tents which provided very little protection against the heavy rains. In the absence of any medical supplies, Major Roberts, Clive and myself could do absolutely nothing for them. We gave them what boiled water we could get from the Jap cook-house, and undertook the dangerous job of mopping up from around them their milk-like excrement, typical of cholera, in which they lay. Yet we had been brought up to these railway camps specifically to tend to the Asian workers, and were kept well away from the Allied P.O.W. areas.

One day, having just returned from the job of supervising the burial of six young Tamils, I felt sick at heart. I halted at the edge of the river and stared into its foaming, yellow-white waters. I fancied I saw reflected in them the appealing eyes of those six young men as they had lain helpless under their flimsy, rain-beaten awnings. Eventually my eyes turned away from the river. I wanted to get away, for the noise was deafening and the sight hypnotic. It was then that I noticed a young man, a P.O.W. like myself, squatting at the foot of a bamboo cluster a few yards away. He was facing the river, motionless, his head buried in his hands. I watched him for some minutes. Then suddenly he sprang up and took a flying leap into the roaring waters below.

Even the two Japanese soldiers who were called to the scene were shaken. Perhaps they, like me, regarded life as precious. Maybe they thought that this English soldier had, after all, done the honourable thing and committed hara-kiri. I shall never know. This awful happening just increased the sickness in my heart, and a wave of hopelessness began to overwhelm me.

Then I found my eyes drawn upwards to what appeared to be a brilliant light. High above, through a hole in the dark ceiling of bamboo leaves, and through a tiny hole in the dark clouds beyond, shone the sun. As I looked, I felt a huge surge within me, and from somewhere deep inside I shouted silently "If only you will save me from this I will never complain again - all I ask is that I have food and clothing." I know now that this was my spirit crying out to God. Somehow after that I found that my courage returned.

The time spent at Hintock was one of the darkest periods of my life. Many times during the day I would hear in the distance the sound of the Last Post, played by a lone trumpeter as the bodies of fellow prisoners were laid to rest. Later I heard many stories about that place, many of which I was unable to confirm. One was that over two-thirds of the original labour force there had died. Originally there had been two camps, one in a hidden valley a few miles away from the main camp. Apparently this came to be known as "Death Valley". The stream that flowed down it, and which at first had been thought would be a good source of water, turned out later to be a carrier of disease. The main work at this place was completed by early August and the three of us were moved a little further up the line. Along with the Jap engineers who accompanied us, we had to build for ourselves a small hut from the bamboo trees that grew around us. Some of these trees had stems up to six inches in diameter, which were ideal for main uprights, particularly for the construction of larger huts such as those needed in the labour camps. In the dry season some Thai men-folk would make a business of travelling up-river in their "pom-pom" boats especially to gather bamboo. They would lash the stems together to form large rafts. From smaller pieces they would construct shelters in which to live as they guided the rafts carefully downstream and back to civilisation.

We completed our small hut in one day, the Jap engineers having provided us with atap covering for the roof and bamboo matting to cover our sleeping area. For the latter we constructed a platform, some eighteen inches high and seven feet wide, down one side of the hut. We soon realised that there was no labour camp near at hand. The Japs used the three of us only for menial jobs, although Clive and I tried as best we could to prevent Major Roberts from doing any manual work. We thought that if we showed respect for him as an officer it might possibly stand us in good stead later.

We had been at our new location only a few weeks when I went down with malaria. It was a particularly nasty form of the sickness, and the symptoms did not match up exactly with those described to us in England during our lectures on tropical diseases. To start with, the fever occurred daily, not every alternate day, or every fourth day. Each day, at dawn, my feet would begin to feel cold and I would then begin to shiver all over, and my temperature would soar. The major and Clive would cover me with their blankets, and gradually I would become less and less conscious of what was going on around me. I remember having the silly idea that I was living in the left side of my brain, and that if only I could get into the right side everything would be O.K.! I still wonder if I had contracted a type of cerebral malaria. After many hours torment I would start to come round, usually by late evening. The fever lasted seventeen days and throughout this time I was unable to eat anything. About half way through my illness Clive managed to buy some tins of condensed milk from some passing Thais - a miraculous happening! At dusk he would heat up a tin with sufficient water to make a drink for the three of us. We had enough for several nights, and the taste of those exquisite bedtime drinks still remains vivid in my memory. At one point I remember thinking that I would never recover. However, my friends later assured me that it had become evident during the last three days of the illness that I was winning through.

One day in early October a remarkable, and to us rather comical thing happened. Our hut was quite close to the railway track, and about a hundred yards up the line from it a railway halt had been established. It was a sunny, hot afternoon (the monsoon had now gone) and suddenly we heard the sound of a diesel loco approaching. As we watched, we could not at first believe our eyes. Behind the loco, in one of two open steel wagons, was a mini-orchestra! The wagon itself was decorated with bunting and lined with mats. Sitting serious-faced behind music stands were musicians, their highly polished instruments glistening in the sun. The loco drew to a halt, and almost immediately we were subjected to a complicated cacophony of strange Oriental music! The sound of brass instruments, woodwind and drums echoed through the jungle, intermingled with the out-of-tune screechings of various stringed instruments. Apparently the Japanese were celebrating the completion of the railway, which made it possible for them to send troops to Burma. The orchestra planned to stop at all the halts on the line in order to share this joyous expression of success with their Nippon brothers! Having told us all this, the Jap engineers then informed us that they would soon receive orders to move many kilometres up the line to a camp just inside Burma. We were to travel with them.

Sure enough, trains carrying troops soon began to travel through, mainly at night. Men who manned the various halts were in contact with each other by telephone. The never-ending ringing of bells and the harsh, agitated voices of the soldiers made it difficult for us to sleep.

A few days later we boarded a train at the halt nearby. As usual, it consisted of several steel wagons hauled by a Bosch diesel loco. I was still very weak from my bout of malaria, and we had no protection from the strong rays of the sun. We had travelled only a few kilometres when an awful hammering noise began. An axle had broken on the wagon in front. In my weak state I had to help transfer all the goods from that wagon into an empty one. I have no recollection of that experience. I probably just worked mechanically in response to the shouts of our Jap masters.

Our journey took us through the highest point of the route, a place known as Three Pagoda Pass. Although an isolated spot, it is marked on the map. Here a gap in the mountains near the source of the Kwai opens the way into south-east Burma. After a journey of about 150 kilometres we reached our destination - a place called Aperon, a labour camp occupied by Allied P.O.W.s.

By this time my body felt completely shattered. In this camp a Welsh medical officer, a man I had known in England, gave me a complete check-over, something Major Roberts for some reason had never done. He told me that my spleen was terribly enlarged as a result of malaria and was protruding well below my ribs. He gave me some tablets other than quinine, which he said were more effective against malaria. I think they were called Atebrin and Plasmoquin. He had managed to keep them hidden away since his capture. Unfortunately, due to the effects of my illness and lack of food I then started to develop beri-beri, the vitamin-deficiency disease caused by lack of vitamin B1. I had severe oedema of the legs and when I pressed my finger into my calves the deep indentation so caused would remain for some minutes.

Just to make matters worse I discovered one day that I had a worm disease - round worm. I had no doubt picked this up from insufficiently cooked pork that had been part of our diet at our last stop in Thailand. The worm had gained entry into my body in the larval stage. When we were attached to the Jap engineers they had given us food from their kitchen, something we were very happy about at the time. The Japs loved diced pork, which they fried in sugar and then boiled with sweet potatoes or other vegetables. Now I was to pay the price for what I had considered then to be a great luxury. When the sergeant in charge of us, whose name was Meoshi, learned that I had contracted round worm he proudly set out to prove that he could deal with it! He had drugs which would eliminate this parasite if and when it was discovered among his own men. First he dissolved in water four ozs. of Epsom Salts, and made me drink it. Then he administered a drug called "Santonin" - a name I have never forgotten! The effect on me was horrendous.

Malaria, with its accompanying high temperature and shivering, returned. I soon had to make frequent trips from my bamboo bed to the latrine outside. I remember my pals having to carry me there on each occasion. When I recovered, I was terribly weak and hardly able to walk. It was then I noticed that my beri-beri had worsened. I now had no feeling in my lower legs - I could pull out hairs and feel no pain at all. I knew that beri-beri could damage muscle and nerve tissue and, if allowed to continue unchecked, could affect heart muscle also. Many prisoners of war had already died as a result of such damage. Happily I was to experience a stroke of good fortune which helped alleviate my condition, if only temporarily.

One day a Jap soldier strode towards me and thrust a glass bottle into my hand. "Use this to make me a lamp", he said, brusquely. No doubt he had chosen me because he knew I would understand him. These crude lamps, mentioned earlier, could be made by taking empty bottles, piercing the screw cap, and threading through them pieces of string. When filled with cooking oil they would burn with a bright yellow flame and give off very little smoke. The bottle was about six inches tall and two inches in diameter. It was full of yeast tablets, most of which were rotten. How glad I was that he had been too lazy even to empty the bottle! I poured out the contents onto a piece of paper and salvaged every tablet that was at all edible and would contain precious vitamin B. I ate the lot without delay and proceeded to make the lamp.

During the night I passed volumes of water. The effect of this was very evident to me next morning. Prior to having taken the tablets I would have guessed that my weight, due to beri-beri, had increased from its normal ten and a half stones to over thirteen stones. Overnight I appeared to have lost half this extra weight. What I did not realise until later was that my true weight at that time would probably have been nearer eight stones, due to prolonged malnutrition and illness. I must still have retained a great deal of water.

I continued to have recurrences of malaria, and my oedema remained. Nevertheless, I regained strength fairly quickly. At the time of our arrival in Singapore I had been in first class physical condition, and this had stood me in good stead. Christmas was only a few weeks off, and Sergeant Meoshi promised us something special for the occasion. Four others of our original medical force had now joined us, and they included two friends from our own unit, and we were delighted to see them. The special treat turned out to be one day off work, plus a special evening meal - some sort of fried rissole! Sergeant Meoshi joined us in this, and afterwards started to sing Japanese songs to us. Unfortunately, his voice was anything but tuneful and we found the music strange. As a result we soon became bored. Sensing this, his manner suddenly changed. Turning to me he said: "Why did you not commit hara-kiri like we brave Nippon troops would have done, rather than be taken by the enemy?". I searched hard for words with which to answer him. Although my Japanese was improving daily, it was still pretty basic. In the event, I made a horrible blunder! What I had intended to say was: "We think that it would be a rather foolish thing to do. We are taught to try to escape so that we can fight again." Later, when I checked in my textbook, I found I had said: "We think that would be the act of an idiot etc...!" His reaction to my statement was instant. Apparently I had ridiculed the sacred Samurai bushido - a code of chivalry sacrosanct to the Japanese. Although later we were to see thousands of Japanese troops surrender to the Allies, we heard of only a few cases of hara-kiri having been committed, mainly by high-ranking soldiers.

Sergeant Meoshi was furious. He drew his bayonet, and I realised that part of him wanted to decapitate us all immediately! Fortunately for us, the other part of him knew that Dr. Matsumoto, his officer-in-charge, would never have allowed it. Instead, he lined us all up outside the hut and told me to tell my friends what I had said. He then proceeded to slap our faces hard. He no doubt thought he had subjected us to a great act of indignity - fitting punishment for our rejection of his Yuletide generosity. Although we had kept straight faces throughout, secretly we had found the incident quite amusing. However, it remained a serious business to Sergeant Meoshi, and I was soon to discover that for me the matter had not ended there. During the next few weeks he would pick on me for no reason, shouting and threatening me in front of his own men as well as my friends. My beri-beri had worsened and I still had shivering bouts as the malaria parasite continued its nasty work in my bloodstream.

One morning I was awakened at first light by a bayonet striking my shoulder. "Get up! You're going to another camp. Pack your kit immediately!". The sergeant was standing over me in an angry mood. He pushed me outside the hut and into the trench that had been dug around it. We never found out if these trenches were intended to protect against rats or whether they were there to offer shelter against Allied planes that by now occasionally strafed the camps. Blows from the blunt edge of the bayonet began to rain on my shoulders. My assailant had assumed an exalted position on top of a mound of earth that had been removed from the trench. He had done this for the benefit of the onlookers; the exercise was fairly harmless and I suffered no real hurt. Having satisfied his ego, Sergeant Meoshi then despatched me immediately to my new destination some twenty or so kilometres further up the line. This brought me nearer to civilisation, to a camp reachable by a mud road from the Burma end of the railway. I found that I was to be alone with a unit of sixteen Japanese engineers. The camp was in a valley at the bottom of which lay the railway line. Straddling the line were three large bamboo huts, and these housed some three hundred Burmese coolies whose job was to maintain the line under the supervision of their Japanese masters. Trees grew on the hillsides, and the engineers were able to fell red teak and other trees suitable for prefabrication of small bridges. There were many of these up and down the line and they provided easy targets for Allied marauding planes, whose activities were now on the increase. A smaller hut stood on the hillside, camouflaged by trees and high bamboo clumps, adjacent to a stream that tumbled down into the valley. Here the engineers lived, and a partition had been made at one end of the hut to provide my sleeping space. This camp was named Konukwei - the place of the seven hills.

The engineers spent most of their evenings drinking raw spirits and wines. These were available to them from a base further along the line. I was subjected to various indignities and taunts, but suffered no physical violence. I was put in charge of sick and dying coolies who were housed in two huts well isolated from the rest of the camp. About fifty sick men were kept here in awful conditions. They had no possessions. They were variously suffering from malaria, tropical ulcer, beri-beri and amoebic dysentery. I was given no drugs, so had no emetine with which to treat dysentery. Those who contracted the disease knew that without treatment they would die, and most became resigned to their fate.

Soon after arrival at this camp I noticed that my beri-beri had worsened. The boost given by the few half-rotten yeast tablets I had come by two months before was beginning to wear off. As I trudged up the hillside back to the hut after each day's work I could hardly drag one foot after the other, and my left thigh had begun to ache badly. I still had bad days in which I experienced high temperature and shivering, reminding me that malaria had not completely gone. Then, one morning shortly after the engineers had left for work, the Japanese cook beckoned me over. A small bamboo cookhouse had been built near the stream, away from the main hut. In the jargon used by most Jap soldiers when addressing P.O.Ws. he suddenly said: "You Kuristianu? You, Paradaiso O.K. ka?". When I replied, yes, I thought I was a Christian, and he found I could speak his language he continued: "We are taught that prisoners of war are less than animals, but I think that all men are equal. What is more, you are bigger people than we are, and need more food!". After this he made sure that I received a good ration of whatever he was allowed to give me. He told me his first name was Watenabe.

Beside each of the engineers' bed space was a bottle of yeast tablets. Over a period of several days Watenabe stood guard whilst I took one tablet from several of these bottles. What our fate would have been had we been discovered does not bear thinking about. With this large source of vitamin B available to me, my beri-beri symptoms gradually disappeared. Soon after this, another unusual thing happened. As I was walking near the railway line one day I quite unexpectedly found myself confronted by Sergeant Meoshi. However, instead of being hostile, he seemed quite pleased to see me. He asked how I was, and when I told him that I still had malaria he produced from his pocket two small bottles containing army-issue anti-malaria drugs. He gave me quite a number of these tablets, instructing me to take two daily. Over the next few weeks my shivering bouts considerably decreased in severity.

At about this time Major Roberts and Clive were sent to join me. Appointed over us was a lance-corporal by the name of Maki, who. was a Jap medical orderly. He was tall for a Japanese, and not very bright. I recall a sickening occasion when, as we walked together through the two long huts occupied by the sick coolies, we came upon a man in his fifties who was in the last stages of amoebic dysentery. He was lying on his back on the ground, obstructing our passage through the hut. As we reached him he said, weakly, and in Burmese: "Water, master". By this time I had learned a few words of the language. Maki asked me what he had said, and I told him. Leaning over, and taking aim carefully, he allowed saliva to drip from his mouth onto the upturned face of the unfortunate man. "Yeh shide", he said in Burmese. "You've got water now". I was furious inside, but impotent to do anything for the man until later. I just hoped then that Maki would one day get his deserts. Strangely, and not very long afterwards, that is exactly what happened.

The incident occurred round about noon one day. The engineers were always out at work on the line from early morning until six in the evening. I had returned to my sleeping space at the end of their hut to collect something or other when I suddenly heard an angry, loudly-raised voice. It was coming from just outside the other end of the hut. I quickly recognised it to be Watenabe's voice. He was shouting orders at Maki, who was standing to attention in front of him. I hid behind the atap partition which separated off my space from the engineers' area and peered between the atap leaves. How pleased I was that by now I understood the Japanese language fairly well! It was soon evident that Maki was the worse for drink, and was being disciplined for it. Watenabe had been left in complete charge that day, and as such was "hancho", and temporarily held the rank of sergeant. Even if a soldier was only a private, if he were made "hancho", as sergeant his word became law to those of inferior rank. Watenabe worked himself up into a rage and finally dispensed an appropriate number of face-slappings, which Maki had to accept in silence. To have answered back would have made things dreadfully worse. Next, Watenabe said to him: "Do you like wine?". "Yes, sir", he replied, very politely and fearfully. As if from nowhere Watenabe then produced a large bottle of Burmese red wine. It was terribly raw stuff.

Watenabe filled a cup to the brim. He held it out to Maki. "Nomi!", he said. "Drink it!"

Maki obeyed, and slowly drank it down. Watenabe filled a second cup which he again handed to Maki.

"Nomi!", he repeated.   Watenabe obeyed, and with great difficulty drank it up.

Watenabe repeated the process, draining the bottle. This time, Maki was unable to cope. Taking the half-empty cup from him, Watenabe threw the rest in his face. He stalked away, leaving Maki whimpering like a child. Later in the day I passed one of the small storage huts in the valley and heard him moaning with pain. His curses were incomprehensible, his speech too slurred to be understood. He did not reappear for two full days.

Towards the end of April the monsoon rains started. When these were at their height water poured down the hillsides in torrents and flooded the bottom of the valley. The rail track remained barely visible. The three of us continued daily to do what we could to help the sick. The Japs also kept us occupied doing chores in their kitchen, one of which was to prepare the fire under the large, saucer-shaped cast-iron dish used for cooking rice. This was about thirty inches in diameter and perhaps a foot deep at its centre. Each evening before dark we washed enough rice for breakfast, put it in the dish with sufficient water, and covered it with a wooden lid. In the morning one of us had to rise early and light the bamboo fire we had prepared the night before. One morning the rain was coming down hard. I gathered my groundsheet around me in order to keep dry as I ran from the main hut to the cookhouse. It was pitch black, but by the light of a match I managed to locate the stack of twigs. Striking another, I bent down to light the fire. As I did so I felt a terrible, stinging pain high up on the inside of my leg. I had been bitten by a scorpion. I caught a glimpse of it scuttling away - it was a black one. It had crawled up the groundsheet, which must have touched the ground as I stooped to light the fire. Like every other prisoner of war on the railway, I was wearing only a G-string. I suffered agonising pain for five hours, and was able to do nothing to relieve it. I shudder to think of the consequences had the scorpion stung me in the scrotal area - I was told that such a sting can be fatal.

July arrived, and with it came some improvement in the weather. One sunny morning Maki asked me to walk with him to the next camp, which was seven kilometres back up the line. I think he just wanted my company, because by now I could speak Japanese quite fluently. Every spare moment that year I had spent reading my text-book. I had greatly improved my grammar and syntax and had amassed a considerable vocabulary.

Our walk up the line was a pleasant one. As we crossed a long, high wooden bridge that spanned a miniature valley, I marvelled at the ingenuity of the engineers who had constructed it without the use of iron girders. They had relied only on clever design and strong joints. Then my heart saddened as I reflected on how many lives must have been lost in the construction of that bridge. It was just one of many similar structures ruthlessly fabricated during the misery of the monsoon rains, regardless of human cost. Eventually we arrived at our destination. Although this was a jungle camp from which escape was impossible, the Japs had nevertheless posted a picket at its entrance from the railway line. Even from a distance I recognised the man on duty. He was an Anglo-Indian sergeant, a man who had been attached to our unit in Changi village around the time I had volunteered to work in down-town Singapore. As we met, my immediate question was: "Any news of my pals? They all left Changi together".

"Bad news, I'm afraid", came the answer. The sergeant was silent for a while. Then he continued: "Their camp was wiped out by cholera last year - polluted water supplies, I believe"... He was going on, giving more details of the tragedy, but I did not hear him. My mind was numb, unable to take in the fact that five men with whom I had shared my life so closely for three years were gone for ever.

It was in this shocked state that I walked back down the line with my escort, Maki. I had no conversation now, I just felt sick inside. Then my mind flashed back to that morning in Changi, and I heard again the staff-sergeant's voice saying, "Two volunteers are needed to work in Singapore city..." A strange shudder went through me. With a certainty I cannot prove, I knew I had been guided away from death, and that Dyson, who had travelled with me on the day of our call-up in 1940, somehow had to die instead of me.

The time came for the engineers to move on. They told us they were going to Sumatra to work on another railway. Just before they left, Watenabe took me to one side and handed me a glass jar. It contained eight ounces of wheat germ; probably a month's ration for his men. As cook, he had been in charge of the food store.

A wagon drew up, and the Japs began to load their kit and themselves into it. Before Watenabe joined them he turned to me and gave me a farewell salute. He did this unashamedly in front of all his friends.

It was half a life-time later, after I had come to know what Christianity was really all about, that I recognised and believed that there had been a purpose behind the events of that Christmas Day in 1943. Only then was I able believe that it had been part of a divine plan to guide me out of danger and to save me from death by disease. Today I am quite certain that God used Watenabe, a Japanese soldier who loved him, to be the means of my deliverance.

5

Interpreter, watchmaker and free man

The camp at Konukwei was taken over immediately by a new team of Japanese engineers. One of the first things we noticed was a deterioration in our rations. I had heard from one of the Burmese coolie headmen who was sympathetic to us that an attempted Japanese invasion of India had failed. Perhaps our new masters were taking it out on us. Before long we did not receive rice from the Japanese cookhouse - we were given instead unpolished rice cooked for the Burmese coolies. I found this stuff pretty horrible.

Round about the end of July we were moved back to Thailand. Our return journey covered almost the full length of the railway. We traversed its many bridges and embankments and clattered through the many cuttings blasted and hewn out of the hostile mountain sides. Had we not been aware of the suffering and death experienced on every mile of the route, that journey would have been an impressive one.

Our destination was a camp on the outskirts of a town called Kanburi, a Japanese simplification of the name Kanchanaburi. It was not a recognised prisoner-of-war camp. In it were housed together Indian coolies, their wives, British prisoners of war and some Japanese soldiers, all of whom had come down from the railway. The camp commander was a fairly old man who we nick-named Papa. He was a cruel man and was drunk most nights. We lived in the usual long bamboo huts, well separated from each other. It was not long before news filtered through that the D-Day landings had taken place. We also had news of Allied prisoners having been shipped to Japan, and that some ships had been attacked and sunk en route. It was not long before we became aware of Allied air activity in our region. Marshalling yards several miles away at a place called Nonproduk were subjected to sporadic attacks. Later they were the target of a night air raid during which many prisoners-of-war were killed unintentionally. The Japs had deliberately built a camp near the yards.

Every day round about noon during that autumn of 1944 the drone of a reconnaissance plane could be heard above us. It was too high to be seen with the naked eye, although we would occasionally catch a twinkle of light reflected from it. Later we were to realise how accurate and detailed the Allies' knowledge of Japanese troop and ordnance locations had become. This was not only the result of air surveillance, it was due also to a highly organised "fifth-column" network operating among the Thais. Every alternate day we P.O.Ws., about 200 of us, would walk to the river to wash and to bring back water. We carried it in what originally had been vegetable cooking oil cans, which were about fifteen inches deep and ten inches square. With a loop of wire across the top we carried them on a bamboo pole, its ends on the shoulders of two of us walking one behind the other. We would put pieces of banana leaf in the containers to stop the water spilling out. Sometimes the Thais, with an eye on the Japanese guard who accompanied us, would drop small pieces of paper into the water. On them would be scribbled the latest war news. Once when we were bathing in the river Kwai a large, low-flying American airplane circled around. Having sorted out a target at the other side of the river it discharged a few rockets and then disappeared. This was our first experience of these new weapons.

I was kept busy both as interpreter and watch repairer. I received a regular trickle of repairs from our guards. They were most deferential towards me and always paid me for my services. With the money I earned I was able to supplement the diet of six of my close friends by buying bananas and duck eggs - the only two items available to us in the camp. We received a small payment weekly from the Japs, enough to buy only an odd item or two. The supply of wheatgerm given to me by Watenabe had lasted until shortly after we arrived at Kanburi. I had more or less ceased to experience malaria or beri-beri symptoms. I was called upon as interpreter many times a day. The first, and most dangerous, time each day was when we collected our daily supply of rice from the store. I would go along with the three men who were to collect the sacks, and engage the guard in conversation. Whenever possible, my friends would empty the contents of an extra sack into the others. One thing we did on a weekly basis was to steal a can of vegetable oil and hide it in one of the rice sacks. Each week we were issued with one tin, sufficient to make a rissole for each of us. This was the sum total of our fat ration. The tins were kept in a hut next to the rice store. There was a considerable number of them and it would have been quite impossible to keep a check on stocks without counting the tins regularly. For many weeks we did this, and remained undiscovered. Then one week we opened a tin and found it to be full of water. What should we do? Was this a trap set for us by the Japs? We knew what could happen if our ruse were uncovered. A short time previously, one of our men who had been employed by the Japs as a driver had been found selling bottles of stolen quinine to the Thais. He had been taken to the local gaol, where they beat and tortured him. He was brought back, gibbering and in chains, and tied to the camp gate. There he remained for two days, during which time the sentries regularly beat him with their rifle butts, before he was taken away to the notorious Bangkok prison. He had been a batman to one of the officers in the camp, and the first thing the officer did when the Japanese surrendered was to dash to Bangkok in order to secure his release.

Another of the few officers who were allowed with us was a fearless character. I remember that he was a dental surgeon and that he once extracted a man's tooth without cocaine! He pulled it out suddenly and unexpectedly, and then with great glee held it aloft for all to see! He persuaded us to take our chance on getting another tin of oil. He and I approached the Japanese corporal together, protesting bitterly, though I myself was trembling inwardly! He asked us to pour some of the tin's contents onto the ground. The clear stream of water slowly emerged. For a second or two he said nothing. Then, with great anger in his voice, he emitted the Japanese equivalent of "What thieving bastards those Thais are!" He then told us to get another tin. I breathed normally again and my trembling diminished.

One thing I learned in my role as interpreter was tact. I was regularly involved in nasty situations arising as a result of bad communication between our men and the Japanese guards. The main cause was the language difficulty. Our captors, of whatever rank, would always address prisoners in the impolite form of their language. They even borrowed words from the Chinese that described us as things rather than people - terribly insulting words in their eyes. All this, of course, was completely wasted on our men. Unfortunately, instead of sticking to the accepted jargon understood by both sides, some prisoners would try to use phrases they had picked up from the guards. These were nearly always very impolite, and their use often resulted in much shouting and face-slapping! The jargon phrases were neutral. The word "Speedo!" always meant "Hurry up!", and because "Benjo" was Japanese for a latrine, then "Speedo banjo" obviously meant diarrhoea! I, on the other hand, had to be able to understand the very impolite army language and be able to reply in the polite form. There are three common forms of politeness in the Japanese language. There is the honorific or very polite form, the colloquial (with a slight difference between male and female usage), and the impolite form - plus Army language! The latter was full of contracted words. Even the word for "is", as in "it is a nice day today", could be "de gozaimasu " (very polite). de arimasu (polite), desu (colloquial), and "da" (very colloquial or impolite). I had to try to use the polite form whenever replying to questions. Thus I developed tact. Mistakes could lead to disaster both for myself and others, especially if the situation was a nasty one, as could occur during regular searches of our huts.

Situated two miles or so from us was the longest bridge over the river. This must have been "The Bridge over the River Kwai", for I never saw another one on my journey up the railway. Originally it had been constructed in wood, a tremendous engineering feat, for the river was quite wide at this point. It had later been replaced by a steel one which I was told had been brought from Java. The line itself ran past our camp only yards away from the perimeter fence. One night I had a vivid dream, every detail of which I was able to remember. I found myself standing in the open space between the two long huts that housed our men. Then, on the near horizon, I saw eleven large planes approaching at a height of about 2,000 feet. I watched them fly towards us. Quite suddenly, when they were less than a mile away they veered to my right and disappeared from sight. At that point I awoke.

The next day at about 2.00 p.m. we were all lined up between the huts ready to be counted before leaving on our regular trip to the river for water and a bathe. Suddenly, eleven planes appeared, flying low on the horizon, exactly as in my dream. The party scattered in panic, looking for shelter although really there was nowhere to go. Yet I remained quite calm, knowing what was about to happen. I stood at the end of one of the huts, watching the planes draw closer. Sure enough, as in my dream, the planes veered to the right. Shortly afterwards we heard the crump of exploding bombs, and explosions continued for several minutes. Obviously the target had been the railway bridge. When, over an hour later, we reached the river we were in time to see railway sleepers and other debris floating downstream. At this point the river swept round the town in a wide curve, and there were beach-like shallows at the place where we bathed. As the debris swept close past us we felt a sense of upliftment and reassurance that we were at last winning the war. These feelings more than compensated for the now noticeable hostile attitude of our guards.

For a long time after that remarkable dream I pondered hard on its origin, implication and purpose. Had it been a psychic happening? If so, what did that say about me? I recalled that my mother had occasionally undergone similar experiences and that she once consulted a spiritualist medium acquaintance in an attempt to uncover the future. What of that strange foreknowledge I had received at the outset of our sea voyage? Our ship had been heading west across the Atlantic and yet I knew we were going to end up in Singapore. Then what about the strange compulsion on that morning parade in Changi village which had led to my friend Dyson having to take my place on that doomed working party late in 1942? Was I being protected or guided in some supernatural way? I could find no real answer to those questions.

The autumn weeks rolled on without our doing any real work at all. The Japanese invented chores for us to do - such as mowing large areas of grass with our hands! Another favourite was making us move huge stock-piles of logs from one side of the road to the other. Then one day we heard on the grape-vine that we were really in transit - the Japs wished to take us to Japan, but their ships were increasingly unable to get through.

In early December our planes dropped leaflets warning of their intention to carry out large scale bombing of Japanese targets on the third anniversary of the attack on Pearl Harbour. Sure enough, at dusk on the 8th of December, low-flying bomber planes suddenly appeared all around us as if by magic. From the shelter of the shallow trenches outside our huts we watched as the aircraft meticulously located their targets. Fires broke out over a huge area, and as the planes passed over us we saw the red glow of the inferno beneath them vividly reflected from their wings. The attack continued for the best part of an hour. Every building occupied by the Japs was hit, although many of them were tightly located between Thai-occupied buildings. The next morning several demoralised Japanese soldiers brought to me their half-charred watches in the forlorn hope that I would be able to repair them!

As Christmas approached, half a dozen of the more musical amongst us formed a small choir, and between us we remembered the words and music of some of the more popular carols. I managed to write the harmonies, and we met regularly at a spot near the perimeter wire for quiet rehearsals. This was the only place out of ear-shot of any occupants of the huts. On Christmas Eve we visited officers and men who were confined to bed through illness, and we sang a few carols at each spot. We believe that the nostalgic, Christmassy atmosphere so created had a therapeutic effect not only on the sick but on the men in general! On Christmas Day itself our cooks did a special fry-up for us. For several weeks they had been conserving their supply of cooking oil especially for the purpose.

Early in the New Year we were moved into a well-established prisoner-of-war camp just a few miles away. A hard-line regime operated there, and we experienced frequent surprise searches of our huts. Our captors sought the least excuse to mete out beatings, which we were all compelled to watch. For example, possession of any non-Japanese currency - even a few cents - was enough to warrant punishment. One officer took sadistic pleasure in this. He would order the "offender" to be bound to a post and then would have him beaten with bamboo rods until he decided the punishment should stop.

A particularly sickening event had taken place on Christmas Eve. One of our men had crawled under the perimeter wire to visit a nearby Thai dwelling at which he knew he could obtain fruit. As he crawled back into the camp bearing a bunch of bananas he ran straight into a Jap sergeant-major who, accompanied by a lance-corporal, was taking a stroll round the camp. This man was notorious for his cruelty. He was small in stature, his legs being so short that the sword hanging from his waist virtually trailed on the ground as he walked. He had a rolling gait, and had been nicknamed by our men "The Rocking Horse". Confronting the frightened prisoner-of-war, he ordered his lance-corporal to shoot him. Getting no immediate response, he shot the Englishman himself.

Such happenings created a sickening feeling in most of us. This feeling was not, I believe, something just borne out of fear and despair, but had more complex roots. It had, I am sure, something to do with coming face to face continually with real evil, under conditions in which we were completely powerless to bring any redress. Terror, anger, hate, frustration and many other emotions were stirred up in us. Such events were bound to have fuelled the deep, repressed fears that we all had about our ultimate chance of survival. It is amazing that depression had not become the norm. Instead, our morale remained high, together with a real camaraderie between us.

I believe that mankind in general has the ability in varying measure to rise above the most adverse circumstances when the instinct to survive calls for it. This does not mean that traumas and stress will have no effect upon us if, by having courage, we appear able to carry on regardless of everything. This truth was made evident to me very soon after moving into the new camp. During my previous six months as camp interpreter I had emerged physically intact from every nasty situation that had come my way. Now, without warning, I found that I wanted to cry. This condition persisted over several weeks. No amount of reasoning could explain why - the desire came from deep inside, a sort of relief as I found I no longer had to set my will resolutely to cope with the unknown happenings of each new day. It had been as if, by so exerting my will, I had been able to draw on a store of inner energy - perhaps my very life - to carry me through those months. That time had ended, and now I was experiencing a sense of weakness and emotional breakdown. It was as if I had been using up my daily supply of nervous energy in advance. Early in the war I had read about bomber crews who had reacted similarly at the end of a long series of missions over Germany.

Eventually my health returned to normal, and I soon got used to my new surroundings in this much larger camp. I found that the food was somewhat better than before. The cooks were most ingenious, and had perfected the technique of baking rice bread. They did this in fired mud ovens, using rice flour which they made by pulverising uncooked rice on flat stones, using large water-filled bottles as rolling-pins.

When it was discovered that I could speak and understand Japanese I was allocated a primitive work-bench within the camp administration hut. One day the whole camp was given a day's holiday. To us this was a remarkable event, for never before had we had a single day off. It was to mark the funeral of a Japanese soldier who had served as a clerk in the office, and whom I had come to know. His name was Yuki-San - Mr. Snow. The Japs, being a fitness-conscious race, had erected a hut specifically for use as a

43

gymnasium. One evening, Yuki had apparently engaged in a wrestling match with a young junior officer. These bouts tended to be of the "no holds barred" type. It seems that the officer had begun to lose a lot of ground. We were later told that Yuki, apparently half drunk, had lost control and really laced into his opponent. At this point the sergeant-major I mentioned previously, The Rocking Horse, had appeared on the scene. Sizing up the situation, he had looked around for a weapon. Nearby was an iron crowbar. Grabbing this, he had struck Yuki from behind with all his force. Writhing in agony from a broken back, the man was taken away and later died of his injuries.

The day after the funeral, as I sat at my repair bench I overheard a conversation between a couple of Yuki's colleagues who were examining his books. "What lovely writing" they said. "What a terrible shame!". They really meant it, yet neither they nor anyone else complained that an injustice had been done. Perhaps they dare not!

Within two months of our arrival at the new site we were on the move again. Many of the original occupants of the camp were now with us, so that our numbers had about doubled. We were taken by wagon to a nearby halt on the railway line. There we were bundled like sheep into closed goods wagons, and without further delay the train moved off eastwards. Shortly after midday the train stopped, and we found that we could travel no further. We had reached a river, and the bridge that had originally spanned it had been destroyed by Allied bombing. It was now spanned by a rope bridge. There were wooden slats to walk on and ropes either side at waist height to hold onto. Carrying our kit on our shoulders, we found the crossing an altogether dangerous business. On the opposite bank were a few decrepit huts that were to be our accommodation for the night. Unfortunately, the cookhouse was on the opposite bank, and to obtain the evening rations some of us had to recross the river. In pairs, we had to make the dangerous return journey

44

whilst carrying the containers of hot rice between us. These containers were of aluminium alloy that measured approximately 20" long x 10" wide by 12" deep, having a carrying handle swung across the top, linked to each end. My companion was a young Dutchman who had been taken prisoner in Java. The container of rice that was issued to us had only half its original handle. It had broken off in the middle, and the other half was missing. My friend was completely unaware that the "hancho" in the kitchen that day was a Jap soldier whom everyone feared. He was known as "The Silver Bullet", because he boasted that, rather than be captured, he would take his own life. He carried a polished bullet around with him for this purpose. His name was Matsumoto Meisan. Foolishly, the Dutchman complained about the broken handle. Matsumoto then started to beat him with a heavy bamboo, and continued to do so for twenty minutes. Occasionally he broke off to strike him with his rifle butt. It was a nauseating display of sadism for its own sake, watched by half a dozen or so other Jap soldiers who no doubt thought it best not to intervene. After all, Matsumoto was "hancho" that day. By the time we left, my Dutch friend was trembling uncontrollably. Later, if he spotted the Korean even at a distance he would shake violently. The next day we were put on another train and eventually arrived at Bangkok. As we reached the city we saw several wrecked locomotives alongside the line, obvious casualties of Allied air raids. Once off the train we were escorted to the river and put on small motor-powered boats. Without delay, these proceeded to chug slowly downstream, taking us past the King's palace, before finally depositing us on the right bank of the river a couple of miles or so further down. When all had disembarked we were escorted into two large, bombed-out warehouses which were to be our new quarters. I remember the large gaping holes in the roof above us through which the bombs had entered. This did not worry us unduly because we were fairly certain that Allied intelligence would be aware of our presence.

We stayed six weeks at this site until we were moved on to what was to be our final destination. Half way through this stay at Bangkok the Japs attempted to move a party of us by night, the reason for which we never understood. We reached the marshalling yards at about midnight; the skies were clear and there was a full moon. After a while we became aware of what we judged to be the sound of heavy bombers several miles away. As the minutes went by this sound seemed to rise and fall. It then grew distinctly louder and we heard planes approaching the city, flying at a height of several thousand feet. At this moment our guards panicked, and pointing to a nearby string of steel railway wagons indicated that they contained ammunition! Then came the command "All men push train!". We had no alternative but to obey, but our efforts were useless, and we began to get a little nervous. The noise of aircraft continued, but soon we realised that they were passing above us in ones or twos, probably returning home from a bombing mission. However, we were still worried in case the marshalling yards might yet be a target. Then a remarkable thing happened. The face of the full moon began to be obscured. Soon we realised that we were watching an eclipse! Moreover, it turned out to be a total eclipse. We waited for an hour or so in the blackness, but rail transport for us did not appear to be forthcoming. Eventually our guards decided to return us to our warehouse base.

When we did finally move from Bangkok we did so late one morning. We travelled in open wagons hauled by the inevitable Bosch diesel loco. It moved eastwards across a monotonous plain, traversing a never-ending, uniform mass of paddi-fields, very few of which were under cultivation. After many hours we stopped at a small town. I seem to remember that the name of the place was Sra-buri. From there we had to march seven or so miles to complete our journey. Our camp lay at the foot of a forested ridge that seemed to cross the horizon as far as the eye could see. Rumour had it that we were not far from the Cambodian border.

The difference between this camp and previous ones was immediately evident. It covered an area of about two acres, was rectangular in shape, and around its perimeter was a mound of earth some ten feet high. At each corner was a look-out tower manned by a soldier armed with a machine gun. A trench twelve feet deep and ten feet wide extended all round the camp, the excavated earth having been used to form the mound. We realised that there was no possibility of escape from here.

The camp was already partly occupied by British and Dutch P.O.W.s. There were six or more large, very long huts of the standard bamboo construction, set out parallel to each other down the length of the camp. A wide open space in front of them acted as a parade area. Everywhere, the ground was sun-baked mud. As usual, the Jap guards' and officers' quarters were set well apart from ours. They were separated from us by an administration hut and stores. From the first day of our arrival I was not allowed to leave camp on working parties, presumably in case I picked up any war news. Instead, I was again given a place in the administration hut and kept occupied with watch repairs. In the absence of any spares I endeavoured to work miracles for my "masters" in an attempt to keep them happy. I had plenty of time in which to do this. I remember once replacing two teeth in a damaged watch wheel. I have no memory of how I did this, for I had no means of soldering! Tension was high in this camp and it was important to preserve as good a relationship as possible with our captors. Unfortunately for me, I was the person through whom all liaison took place! Hut searches were frequent, even to the point of occasionally digging up the ground if it were suspected that earth had been disturbed. This practice really began in the early days of our captivity, when ingenious radio engineers had concealed miniature receivers in all sorts of places. Sometimes they fitted them into the bottom half of an army issue water bottle, sometimes they hid them below ground. Men who had been caught had been executed. I suppose it was logical for the Japs to believe that, as the only watchmaker in the camp, I had watches hidden somewhere amongst my kit or nearby. One day they spent a solid hour searching around my sleeping space. Actually I did have a few watches hidden inside one of the bamboos that formed part of the hut's outside wall! It was one of the supports to which was attached the matting screen that was made from long. interwoven, wide shavings of bamboo. Such matting was used for screens round latrines, for the walls of huts, and for our sleeping area. The bamboo in question was quite near to where I slept. It was an open-ended piece about three inches in diameter. Its top was about three feet above the sleeping space, behind my head. There was a gap between it and the roof. The watches were suspended from a piece of thin string to a point eighteen inches down the inside of this bamboo. As I watched the search from a distance, my pulse raced. I thought it would never end. Fortunately, Japanese Oriental cunning was outmatched by British Western ingenuity, and they finally gave in! I dread to think what would have happened to me had my ruse been uncovered. Not long before, men had already been severely beaten for far less serious offences.

Each morning all fit men were lined up, counted, and marched off to work. An air strip was being constructed at a site not far from the camp. Our rations were very basic and life was monotonous, but such things were nothing new. They were insignificant, in fact, compared with our constant preoccupation with what might happen to us in the weeks ahead. In a couple of months the monsoon would be gone, and from news we had picked up whilst in Bangkok it seemed possible that our forces might then invade Malaya. Isolated as we were, caught like rats in a trap, we envisaged ourselves being mown down as the four machine guns that overlooked the camp were turned on us. Our bodies could then be conveniently thrown into the deep trenches already in existence. We tried to think up a means of escape. Our best idea was that we should hide below ground in the latrines. I reckoned that for the plan to succeed we would need to devise some type of gas mask!

The weeks dragged by, and once again clear blue skies became the norm. July came and went, with no news of happenings in the world outside. Then, one day in mid-August, the men who had left for work that morning returned before noon. They reported that the Japs had been burning papers and smashing up bottles of booze at the work site. We guessed that something significant must have happened.

I still had work to do in the administration hut. A smaller building nearby was the camp commandant's office. About mid-afternoon, on hearing voices coming from that direction, I glanced up from my work to see what was happening. I could hardly believe what I saw. A large map was spread across the desk, and peering into it was the camp commandant and a British Guards Officer. The latter was a well-built, tall man who held the rank of major. Standing nearby was a British army sergeant. Both Englishmen carried revolvers at their waist, and the sergeant had a string of hand-grenades strapped round him. About twenty minutes later I was called over to them. I was informed that the war was over and that the Japanese had surrendered. I was ordered to instruct our bugler to sound reveille. This had never happened before. Each morning, a Jap soldier had sounded a reveille which bore no similarity to the British version.

Our man took up his position at the centre of the parade area. When reveille was sounded, the response was dramatic and emotional. As the news spread among the men, many were filled with disbelief. Some were even scornful. As the truth of the news sunk in, many broke down in tears. Some Dutchmen cried unashamedly. When the uproar had settled down, the British officer mounted a rostrum that had been used occasionally by the Japanese to make special announcements. He brought us up to date with the news, explaining how the Japanese surrender had been the outcome of our atom bomb attacks on Hiroshima and Nagasaki. He told us to remain fairly quiet over the next few days, and advised us not to sing the National Anthem or loud patriotic songs. Armed Japanese troops still occupied sites in the wooded area on the hillside behind the camp, and obviously it would be unwise to provoke them.

He told us how extensive preparations had been made within the country for a possible invasion by Allied forces. Officers had been dropped into areas of Thailand unoccupied by Japanese troops, and a considerable army of men had been trained for action should an invasion have taken place. He set out next day to visit the Japanese army headquarters in the hills. He went alone and unarmed, to accept their surrender. As far as I know, he managed to do this without difficulty. Meanwhile, I was able to speak to his sergeant. I was amazed to discover that he came from my own home town!

We were unable to leave the camp immediately. Due to a

49

smallpox outbreak in the area we were to be quarantined for a month. Naturally, this came as a big disappointment to us. However, many things occurred that made the days pass quickly. Straight away, our diet improved dramatically. Vegetables arrived by the cartload, and we saw real meat, albeit tinned, for the first time in years. After a week or so every prisoner in the camp was subjected to questioning by a special unit that had been flown in for the purpose. To do this, tents were erected on the parade area. We were interviewed individually, and sworn statements were taken from us concerning any atrocities we had witnessed or heard about. I told my first-hand story of Matsumoto Meisan's cruel beating of the Dutchman, and related what I knew of the murder of our fellow-prisoner by the Rocking Horse on the previous Christmas Eve.

A few days later we heard that one of our light planes had managed to land on the almost completed airstrip. We were given a few hours in which to write letters to our folks before the plane was to take off again. We crammed three and a half years of news into half a dozen thin pages. I knew my letter would be both a joy and a shock to my mother and father when it reached them. They had received no news of me since the fall of Singapore.

About half-way through the quarantine period Lady Mountbatten arrived at the camp. She first made a tour of the huts, shaking our hand and having a brief word with many of us. Some sort of stage was erected on the parade ground from which she could address everybody. She told us that a Labour Government had been elected, and this raised loud cheers from most of the crowd. Not being a political animal, this news did not affect me greatly. However, she shared with us much other information that interested us all considerably. We were hungry to know what had gone on in the outside world during those years lost to us. One thing that astounded us was the invention of the jet engine. That this could be true we found difficult to imagine. Hitherto such things had only been the stuff of schoolboy comics.

By now there was quite a bit of air activity in our area. Earlier we had seen only the isolated plane, which we believed was searching

50

for camps like ours. One had returned, and flying low, had dropped parcels of Virginia cigarettes and English newspapers. I thought the journalistic quality of the latter had fallen considerably - my personal opinion, of course! Sentences were shorter and simpler.

Now that our diet had improved, many of us concentrated on getting fit. Along with others I spent some time each day running round the parade ground. Having no running shoes, we ran in bare feet. The hard mud surface was fairly kind to us. It was reckoned that seven times round the course was about one mile. The performance of most of us improved rapidly, and we decided to hold a one mile race in front of the whole camp. I amazed myself by winning this with a lap to spare. From an early age I had enjoyed running. I'm afraid I was fairly useless at sport. From boyhood I had found running extremely enjoyable and exhilarating. I loved the thrill of flying like the wind down hills. In training after my call-up I had entered my Divisional long-distance running competition and had been one of the front runners. I was pleased now to find that my muscles appeared to have survived the ravages of beri-beri and other diseases.

The day finally came when we loaded our kit-bags into army wagons and were driven (by a Japanese) to Bangkok airport. As soon as we arrived we were given things we had never ever seen in captivity - toilet soap, a toothbrush, oranges and the like. Several Dakota aircraft were awaiting us; each would carry twenty-five men. The pilot of my plane was a Yorkshireman with long experience of flying Dakotas. He told us that our destination was Rangoon, and that immediately after take-off he would look for a gap in the clouds and try to get above them. Apparently they could become electrically charged by the sun, and already two or three planes had touched them and been knocked out of the sky. What horrible luck, I thought, to have survived three-and-a-half years as a prisoner of war and then to be killed in that way. As we headed westwards, climbing steeply to get above cloud level, we found ourselves flying above the mass of jungle that had been our home two years before. Occasionally we caught the sun's reflection from the River Kwai, at places at which the river was wide enough to be seen between the overhanging masses of bamboo thicket. There were no seats in the aircraft. A couple of empty fifty gallon oil drums travelled with us, and the floor of the fuselage was black with oil. We guessed that the plane had been used for ferrying fuel. The pilot had told us that because of our great height the atmosphere would be rarefied, but this did not trouble us. Eventually we left the land behind us, and saw below the outline of the Bay of Bengal. A mile or two from the shore, we could see where the sea depth suddenly increased. No longer was the sunlight reflected from the yellow sea bed. Everywhere, the ocean was dark blue. Then we spotted in the distance the Shwei Dagon Pagoda. It towered above the city of Rangoon, its golden pinnacle reaching towards the sky.

There was no runway available at Rangoon's main airport, and we landed on a temporary airstrip on the outskirts of the city. When we emerged from the airplane we were greeted by young W.A.A.F. personnel. To us, these girls all appeared beautiful! We were showered with gifts and affection. After partaking of food and drink we were taken to a hospital in the city. Those who were ill with dysentery or malaria were put to bed in the medical wards. The rest of us were given beds in adjacent rooms. I enjoyed a wonderful sleep that night. Next day we were fitted out with new tropical uniforms and later were given a complete medical examination. I was issued with a supply of anti-malaria drugs sufficient to last until we reached England. One day we received a surprise visit from Lord Mountbatten of Burma. He sat with us in our room and chatted for half an hour. He recounted stories, some horrendous, of how our troops had flushed out the Japanese in upper Burma. No doubt he thought this would gratify our desire to take revenge on our former captors. Yet for many like myself these stories merely reinforced the horrors of war, which we longed to forget.

We stayed in Rangoon about a fortnight, and I had an opportunity to visit the Shwei Dagon Pagoda. I went along with two friends, and before ascending the long flight of stone steps that led to the entrance, we had to discard our shoes. Visitors could leave their footwear at the foot of these steps without any fear of it being stolen. In the outer chambers of the building dealers in semi-precious stones - mainly rubies, sapphires and emeralds - displayed their wares for sale. At the centre of the building were several large statues of Buddha, and two or three yellow-robed monks stood by, willing to answer any questions we put to them. At one side we spotted two young men sitting together in a corner, arms around each other's shoulders, behaving like young lovers. Pointing at them, one monk said: "There you see the outworking of Karma; that is the result of their wrong-doing in a former life". In another place we saw a class of students receiving instruction from an older monk. The outside of this huge pagoda appeared to be covered in gold leaf -whether or not this is really the case I am not certain. We were assured that in the pinnacle of the spire was a casket of jewels worth millions of pounds.

At the end of our stay in Rangoon we were put aboard a Dutch vessel, together with some two thousand other ex prisoners-of-war. I found the journey down the Irrawaddi delta fascinating. We were piloted down the main channel either side of which were other channels separated by long fingers of land. These appeared almost awash with water, like giant tentacles projecting outwards from the mainland. We headed south into the open sea, and then turned westwards towards home. I did not sleep in my bunk, preferring to stay up on deck after dark. I remember well the beautiful star-lit nights spent lying there, enjoying my freedom, with the gentle, warm sea breezes fanning my face. Each night, the constant, soft swish of the ship's wash would eventually soothe me to sleep. Several days later we reached Sri Lanka, then called Ceylon. We were to berth at Columbo overnight. It was almost dark when the island appeared on the horizon. Whilst still a mile or two out to sea the sky suddenly become a mass of light, as searchlights from ships in the bay criss-crossed above us. At the same time, our ears were subjected to an explosion of sound from the ships' sirens. Long, repeated, variously pitched blasts sounded a noisy, but to us joyous note of welcome. Vessels of every size and nationality had joined in this unanimous salute to our freedom.

We left port next morning, all of us having received a present - a pound of Ceylon tea. I remember little of the next stage of our journey, except that it was during that time that I wrote a letter to Agnes, who was later to become my wife. Our teenage romance had ended just before the war, yet now I felt that I had to write to her. When we reached Aden all our mail was flown home. As we sailed up the Red Sea and into the Suez Canal we passed the sunken hulks of bombed shipping that littered the small lakes that form part of this waterway.   Soon we were traversing the Mediterranean. We passed the rock of Gibraltar at 1.00 a.m. so I saw nothing of it. I could just make out a misty triangular outline that enclosed a host of twinkling lights. A day later we handed in our tropical kit and were issued with the U.K. army uniform so familiar to us during our training period in Britain.

Our ship docked in Liverpool at the end of October. The skies there looked dark and sombre. I decided that this was because it was autumn, although, strangely, the weather was quite clear. Then it dawned upon me that it was more than that. I had been used to intense sunlight for over three and a half years, and the contrast was marked. We stayed overnight in barracks, and at nine o' clock next morning left for home. With me in the railway carriage was a friend called Joe Binns, who had travelled to Norwich with me on the day of my call-up in March, 1940. Three other conscripts had been with us on that day, and we both realised with sadness that all had died on the Burma railway. I was overwhelmed with a sense of thankfulness that I was still alive. We both lived just outside Bradford in West Yorkshire, a couple of hours journey from Liverpool. It was Sunday, and when we left the railway station at the end of our journey, the city seemed dead. We soon located a taxi rank. Our homes lay in different directions and, excitedly, we shook hands and said our goodbyes. As my taxi driver loaded my kit-bag into the car boot, I settled down into the passenger seat, my heart pounding as we set off on this very last stage of my journey home. Many times during those years of captivity I had imagined this homecoming, and had lived out in fantasy a joyous, longed-for reunion with my parents and sister. As we travelled along the main road out of the city, it was as if I were viewing the scene from above. It all seemed unreal, too good to be true. It seemed no time at all before the taxi entered my street.

A moment later my mother was embracing me.

6

Homecoming, marriage and strange happenings

The letter I had written from the prisoner-of-war camp in Thailand had taken just a couple of weeks to reach home. The shock of receiving it had caused my mother to lose her voice. Now, as we gained control of our tears, and as the joy of our reunion subsided, I realised that she had still not fully recovered. I entered the house and fell into the arms of my father and sister. I saw immediately the evidence of years of worry written plainly on my parents' faces. We began to exchange news. During the three and a half years of my captivity I had not been allowed to write home. Because of that, my family had not known whether or not I was still alive. My father spoke of the countless nights during which conversation had turned to wondering about where I was and how I might be. On such occasions all attempts to find sleep had been useless. Whilst at Kanburi in late 1944 I had received from home several postcards at once. They had been posted at intervals over the previous two years. Heavily censored, they had contained no real news, but most of them had reassured me that my family was still in good health.

I tried to pick up life where I had left off before the war. My reunion with Agnes was very special; after nearly five years we had both changed. Throughout those years I had remembered her as a teenager, but now she was twenty-four years old, and a mature woman. The realisation had sent a tingle down my spine. As we embraced, we knew that a real love for each other had survived those years. Feelings of joy and happiness, long forgotten, began to

56

flood back into my life. Not many weeks later I proposed to her. She accepted, and soon afterwards we were engaged to be married. Physically, the new Agnes appeared to me lovelier than ever. Her head of auburn hair, so attractive to me in my teens, still crowned her now slim, but well-covered figure. I, on the other hand, presented a somewhat gaunt appearance. I had not yet completely recovered from the effects of malnutrition, and a staring look in my eyes bore evidence to the trauma I had undergone during those years away.

Within a week of returning home I enquired about my old job. For four years prior to my call-up I had worked in a laboratory based at the local sewage works. There the purification process was monitored and drinking water analysis and bacteriological examinations carried out. Atmospheric pollution was recorded by monthly analysis of the local rainfall, and occasional checks on river pollution were undertaken. I really had not wanted this job, and would have much preferred to have taken up journalism. My parents, however, conditioned by their experience in the depression of the 1930s, had wanted a more secure job for me. This particular position had depended on the outcome of my final school exams.

After a year of hard study I had achieved higher grades than the others on the short list. I had worked especially hard because my mother had taken up part-time domestic work in order to keep me at high school. The job would involve my doing an external B.Sc. degree course in chemistry - not my best subject. I much preferred the arts. However, the chief laboratory assistant, who had a perverted sense of humour, had assured me that there was a lot in sewage! He had said that the possibility existed of my becoming manager of a large city works and achieving a big salary. In the event, my parents had refused to let me have any say in the matter.

I discussed the possibility of an early return to work with my former boss. As the works manager, he was highly qualified chemist. Lancashire bred, and in his forties, I had found him fairly easy to get on with. Sadly, his wife had been an invalid for a number of years. He told me that, as yet, the laboratory was not fully staffed, and my job was still open. Nobody was employed to undertake the regular quantitative analysis of sewage and effluent upon which control of the purification works depended. Examination of the town's drinking water must have been carried out elsewhere. The only other member of staff now employed was a forty-five year old lady secretary, who also acted as wages clerk and book-keeper. She happened to be the wife of my former chemistry master.

My boss painted a dismal picture of my future, should I wish to stay in the sewage business. No longer, apparently, was there a lot in it. Although I had, at twenty-one, qualified as an Associate Member of The Institute of Sewage Purification (the youngest person ever to do so, apparently), it now appeared that a degree was vital if I was ever to get a manager's job. At the time I had no knowledge of government assistance available to those in my position who had returned from the war. Neither did I remember that I possessed the Matriculation Certificate of London University which would have opened the way to a university degree. My A.M.Inst.S.P. qualification was just not enough; anyway, sewage had become an embarrassing word. It was not long before every sewage works in the nation adopted the apparently more positive and less amusing title of "Water Pollution Prevention Department".

The final discouragement came when my boss revealed how meagre my salary would be if I stayed in my old job. Agnes and I planned to get married in the spring, and I needed to be able to support her. She would give up her job as secretary at the local electricity works. Her office was not far from our works laboratory, and it was because of this that we had first met. As teenagers we had walked the same couple of miles to work each day. We had formed a friendship that had blossomed into romance. Because of the war, six years had been lost to us. In the period when we were coming out of adolescence into adulthood, and when we were at the peak of physical fitness, those years could have been the happiest of our lives. Now, the discovery that my career plans apparently could not be fulfilled plunged me into bewilderment. I was not to know that salaries were soon to be substantially reviewed, and that the outlook for me was not the bleak one that my boss had portrayed.

A few days later I bumped into a friend from the past - the man who had taught and trained me in the craft of watchmaking. Donald was a brilliant repairer and the fastest worker I have ever known. Before the war he had been the manager of a watch repair materials business, a local firm that had grown to become one of the two largest watch materials wholesalers in the country. During the war years the firm had turned to precision engineering, making special parts for the Ministry of Defence. Now, Donald had decided to go into business on his own as a watchmaker to the trade and as a retail jeweller. He invited me to become his partner. He assured me that the time for this joint venture was exactly right. He said that there was more work and more money awaiting us than we could ever imagine. His plan was to open a combined shop and workshop in a local village. Returning home, I sat down with Agnes and pondered the matter. It seemed that an income would be assured; I would receive further expert guidance and training from Donald, and we would be independent of bosses. Being self-employed, I told myself, was itself worth many pounds per week. Moreover, because Agnes and I had both contributed to the local government's superannuation scheme, we would receive considerable cash if we gave up our jobs. We could then use this money as the deposit on a house. After much thought and discussion I agreed to take up Donald's offer. So within a few weeks of my return home I found myself working full time in a job that demanded a great deal of nervous energy. In retrospect, I came to realise that it had been a most foolish thing to do. Not only was my nervous system in a weak, damaged state, but the full reaction to my return home from the Far East had not yet set in. By comparison, my job in the sewage works laboratory would have been child's play. Yet I loved watchmaking, and looked forward to an exciting future alongside my friend.

Shortly before our wedding the following April, Agnes and I called one evening at a popular country inn situated on the edge of the Yorkshire Dales. As we sat in a corner of the lounge we noticed a couple at the other end of the room. Somehow, they seemed familiar. They sat snuggled together, intimately engaged in conversation. After half an hour or so they rose to leave. It was then that we recognised them. My old boss, smartly dressed, walked past us, his secretary on his arm. Her blonde hair, carefully styled, contrasted strikingly with her vividly made-up features. Obviously they were having an affair - and in no way had either of them wanted me back in my old job. Their cunning deception had served to alter the course of my life.

Immediately upon my return home I resumed my place in the local church choir. At the age of twelve my mother had persuaded me to leave Methodism so that I could become a choirboy in the Anglican church. They did not, of course, attend church themselves. I still ponder the motives of parents of that generation who sent their children to church. Was it just to get them out of their way, or did they somehow believe that they were really being influenced for good?

I was surprised to discover that my parents had attended church from the time they had received the telegram from Singapore. It seems that my vicar had visited them and invited them to take Holy Communion. Apparently they had been so thankful to know that I was alive that they accepted the invitation. They had continued to attend regularly after that. I took up my old role as choir-member because I enjoyed the four-part singing and I loved the company of my old friends. I never really doubted, I suppose, that I was a Christian, and the reality of my faith had never been challenged by anyone.

I remember a strange experience I had during the first choir rehearsal after my return home. As our choirmaster guided us step by step through a particularly difficult piece of music, it was as if I was suddenly lifted out of the group and became a spectator. Fearful thoughts began to occupy my mind, such as: "They are spending all this time trying to get this piece of music note-perfect, but they don't realise that half the world is starving, and that we need to do something about it without delay. Don't they know that now we have the atom bomb the whole world could soon be blown to pieces?" - and then suddenly I found myself back on earth and part of what was going on. I had no idea what was happening to me. When I told my doctor he said that these were probably symptoms of anxiety neurosis. In clinical terms he was no doubt right. Much later I came to understand the spiritual causes that really lay behind what had happened.

I was now full of physical energy and drive, and was enjoying setting up in business with Donald. The rather staring look in my eyes that had appeared since my return home apparently still persisted, and Agnes would mention it from time to time. It was more noticeable when people asked me to relate my prisoner-of-war experiences.

After Christmas, Agnes and I started to look seriously for somewhere to live. We found a small semi-detached house which was only a couple of miles from our home town, and about the same distance from our business premises. I suppose I was working flat out during those first ten weeks of 1946, both at business and in preparing our new home. We had experienced no difficulty in obtaining a Building Society mortgage, and interest rates were only four per cent at that time. I worked late each day on the huge pile of watch repairs that had already accumulated in our workshop. Then, when our house became vacant, I also began to work late in the evenings, decorating walls and ceilings and doing other essential jobs. After a while I began to feel the stress of all this effort. Whether or not that had anything to do with the following strange experience, I cannot say.

One afternoon I was working alone at the watch-bench. Donald had gone to the watch materials suppliers, and the door of our premises was locked. We had become so busy that we had decided to open for trading only three days per week. The job of watch repairing demands intense concentration, and requires perfect co-ordination of hand and eye. Yet it needs little thought. Assembly of watch movements, something achieved through a combination of feel and sight, can be done when the mind is "miles away" and is thinking about something else entirely. One may perhaps just stare at the work and have no thoughts at all. Maybe that is how I was that afternoon.

Without warning, I found myself not just a withdrawn, external viewer of a scene, as I had been at that first church choir rehearsal. This time I was actually outside my body, looking at it from a point some ten feet away. I was viewing myself from behind, looking at the back of my head, watching myself assembling a watch. Needless to say, I was terrified. My urgent desire was to get back into my body. For that reason, the whole experience lasted only a couple of seconds. I did not look to see if I did in fact possess another body, but I do know that my mind and reason were operating out there, and that my will was there also. I remember that it was through exerting my will that I had rapidly re-entered my body. The whole thing had been a quite involuntary and spontaneous happening. I have since learned that this experience is not uncommon, and that very many recorded accounts exist of happenings similar to my own. Researchers have written books on the subject. Apparently people from all walks of life have recounted similar experiences. Often they had occurred immediately after road accidents. Sometimes it had been a sudden involuntarily happening, as in my own case. For others the experience had occurred during a time of very serious illness. Apparently the phenomenon is known as "excursion of the soul", or "the out-of-the-body experience". I was, in fact, to have a similar, yet different, experience later, and for this reason I will not write more about the subject here.

Agnes and I had arranged for our marriage to be held in church on 27th of April that year - rather less than six months after my return home. It took place on the first Saturday after Easter. We had a great send-off from a host of well-wishers, parents and friends, and numerous relations. The red carpet literally was put down for us, covering the church steps as we left by the west door. In those days the verger curiously had in his possession a wide roll of red carpet which he made available for weddings at an appropriate fee! We were greeted by cheering friends, photographers and confetti. The church bells rang out for us a recorded peel of rejoicing! Agnes

62

and I left fairly quickly for the local portrait photographer's studio, before moving on to receive our eighty or so guests at the wedding reception.

Right up to the day of our wedding I had worked long hours both at business and in our new house. Now I was determined to relax and enjoy our honeymoon. We set off from the local railway station in mid-afternoon, our parents and friends cheering and waving goodbye from the platform. I recall vividly the overwhelming happiness I experienced as we began our journey together. We were oblivious of all but ourselves, completely in a world of our own. To make things even more perfect, we occupied an empty compartment in a barely half-filled train. We looked forward to this first week of our new life, based at a modest boarding house in the Lancashire seaside resort of Morecambe. As we left the station the sun shone down on us from a clear blue sky. Even nature seemed to be blessing us.

We were able to take advantage of the dry, fairly warm weather that was set to continue right through our week away. The Lake District was within easy reach by coach, and in those days Morecambe itself had quite a lot to offer, even though the holiday season had not yet begun. The week flew by quickly, and our thoughts began to concentrate on establishing our new home. Our semi-detached house was quite small, and was built on a hillside in the Aire valley at the bottom of the dale, about eight miles from Leeds. The small, private estate stood in an elevated position. Just a few miles away were wooded hills, and behind them heather-covered moors stretched out into the distance. We liked the brightness of the place, and we were to enjoy living there. That is, despite the one or two strange happenings that occurred during our stay. What!, you say, not again! Not more queer events! Sorry! I too did not understand them at the time, or why these things seemed to follow me around.

We had managed to furnish only part of the house. The deposit needed for the property had left us with only a small amount of cash for essentials. This we had used to furnish and decorate the lounge and the larger of the two bedrooms. The small bedroom, which was at the back of the house, was still untouched when we returned from our honeymoon. In the centre of the uncarpeted wooden floor sprawled a pile of old watch cases almost a foot high and about two feet in diameter. I had accumulated these watch cases during my teenage years. In those days one could purchase broken watches in the city markets very cheaply. Before our marriage I had transported these empty cases in suitcases from my parents' house and dumped them in the empty bedroom. It was about midnight on that first day in our new home. We had been in bed only a short time, relaxing in each other's arms, as newly-weds do. Suddenly, interrupting the silence, we heard the sound of the rear bedroom window being opened. The handle of the steel-framed window was about halfway up on the inside, and was very stiff. The squeaking and grating noise which we knew occurred when this window was opened was followed by what appeared to be the sound of heavy boots hitting the floor. Immediately afterwards there was a crashing, metallic sound, the loud noise of watch cases being scattered as if someone had walked straight through them. I jumped out of bed in an instant, switching on all the upstairs lights. I flung open the small bedroom door, expecting to be confronted by a burglar. To my amazement, the room was empty. Nothing had been disturbed. Agnes had heard exactly what I had heard. For twenty-seven years up to that time I had remained a down-to-earth, practical person, as you may have gathered already. Occurrences like this just had to have a practical explanation. Physical laws just could not be broken. I had spent four teenage years studying science, and as a watchmaker and precision engineer I knew those laws to be absolute. Yes, I appeared to have received guidance and protection during my time as prisoner-of-war, but that was still a mystery to me. I knew nothing of metaphysical happenings; neither had I investigated the paranormal. On the other hand, you who are reading this may be aware of these things. You may believe in poltergeists. I ask you to be patient and to read on. For during fifty years following this event, beginning with foolish curiosity which led to much suffering, the enormity of a battle that exists between good and evil and which embraces supernatural happenings such as I have related has been made real to me. This battle, which is for our souls, is hidden from most people because it takes place in the supernatural realm. You may not accept this, or acknowledge the existence of God, or of Satan. Yet I encourage you to pursue my story to its end. Allow me to share how I was made aware of the reality and scope of this supernatural, spiritual dimension. You may then judge for yourself.

7

Depression strikes -
a spiritist "heals" me

Agnes became pregnant at the beginning of June. This was not planned, but we looked forward with excitement to the happy event, as did all our parents. It was at about this time that I had a second "out of the body experience" similar to the one I mentioned earlier. This time it occurred when I was in bed. The lights were off and I was lying on my back. Again, without warning, I found myself floating upwards towards the ceiling, and I was frightened. The difference between this and my earlier experience was that, although my bedroom had been completely dark, now it was bathed in a purple light. I could see round the room, through the windows, and beyond. I knew that, had I wanted to, I could travel outside into space and visit places far away from that room. I believe that because I was frightened, I "willed" myself quickly back into my body.

Another strange happening occurred a month or two later. Lying in bed one night, we both felt the bed tilt gently sideways to an angle of about thirty degrees, and then back again. We thought a land subsidence must have taken place. In the past there had been such occurrences in the district due to a geological fault known as the Craven Fault, situated higher up the Aire valley. Next morning we hurried round to see if our neighbours were all right. They were an elderly couple. They had experienced nothing. Our phantom intruder had struck again. We racked our brains in an attempt to understand what might be going on. Could my "out of the body experiences" be linked to the two poltergeist type happenings in

66

our new home? Of course, we had read about such things, but had given no more credence to them than we had to ghost stories. For neither of us had such happenings ever been part of our experience. We made enquiries of local residents concerning previous owners of our house, which had been built in the early nineteen-thirties. Apparently the couple from whom we had bought it were Jehovah's Witnesses. A very elderly resident in the district could remember that an old, long-since demolished farmhouse had once existed on the approximate site of our home. He said that years ago it had been the scene of a murder, suicide, or both. We never made sense of all this, and ceased to worry about it. Very many years later I was able to discern more clearly the possible causes of our strange experiences.

By this time, Donald's marriage had broken up and he had moved to London. We had agreed a price for his business, and were to pay him by making monthly deposits into his building society account.

Our daughter Margaret was born at the end of the following March. She was a lovely, dark-haired baby, and everyone agreed that, in facial appearance at least, she "took after" my side of the family! Often, when I arrived home for lunch, she would be asleep in her pram outside the house. I would peep in at her, and a great feeling of happiness would overwhelm me. Then, one lovely sunny day, as I looked down into the pram, a thought suddenly entered my mind: "This is too good to be true, it can't last." Fear and panic overtook me. From that time on, a feeling of inner darkness and depression took hold of me. I literally felt myself to be in a dark tunnel. I thought I could see a light at its end, yet however hard I tried I was unable to reach it. My doctor prescribed various medications, mainly barbiturate based, but none had any effect. I tried to reason why I should be in this darkness of depression, but found no logical answer. Here I was, freed from captivity and happily married, with a baby girl, and living in our own house and running our own business. I could make no sense of it all.

I continued to visit my G.P. regularly for almost a year. He tried everything - tonics, more barbiturates, pep talks, and psychology with a little bit of suggestion thrown in. I believe that his expectations were that his neurotic patient would one day spontaneously recover. Unfortunately for both of us, that did not happen. Eventually the time came when he told me that if I did not "snap out of it" he would have to refer me for psychiatric treatment.

It was at that point that Jane, a twenty-one year old friend who attended my church, approached me with an offer of help.

"Jack", she said, "my father has a friend who has a very special gift, and he is sure he can help you". "Well", I replied, somewhat scornfully, "my doctor has tried every means imaginable for almost two years without success, so what makes you think that a layman can possibly help me?"

I had no desire to pursue the matter. I found it absurd that any unqualified person could be of any use. Yet Jane persisted, and eventually persuaded me to meet her father. He turned out to be a likeable person.

"Although my friend Bob is quite ordinary and is well-known in the textile industry, he does have a remarkable gift", he said. "In fact, he spends most of his free time helping people". He spoke with such certainty that I eventually gave in. I made an appointment to meet Bob at his office the following week.

About fifty years old, tall, with receding hair, Bob welcomed me warmly. "Take a chair", he said. "Because you don't know anyone I've helped, I suppose I'd better sell myself to you."

"Tell me what you can do that my doctor can't!", I replied instantly. My question had a note of challenge about it. "Are you a Christian Scientist or something?"

"Oh no!", he came back quickly. "But since childhood I've had a rather supernatural gift which I now use to help others."

"Really", I replied incredulously. "And just how does it work?" It has always been my nature to want to know the last detail of everything.

He began to explain. He said he had come to see that we are, if

68

you like, a perfect reflection of an inner self, which he would call our unconscious self. When he decided to help people who really wanted to be helped, he said that a power flowed through him which was "consistent with all that is good'. This power, he assured me, would erase all the damage I had received during my years as prisoner-of-war, and I would be cured of my depression. It all sounded very strange to me. Yet what had I to lose? I arranged to visit his home the following evening.

I arrived at Bob's house promptly at 7.30 p.m. As I entered, a young man was just leaving. I wondered if Bob had been helping him, too. When his guest had gone he lit up a cigarette, and his wife brought him a cup of tea. I noticed that his face looked somewhat drained. We chatted for about ten minutes and then Bob asked me to accompany him to a room upstairs. This room, he told me, was reserved especially for his work with people like myself. He asked me to lie on the bed and relax. He sat on a chair nearby, and closed his eyes. After a while I thought I heard him counting quietly – then there was silence. A few minutes later he began to address my "unconscious self" as if it were another person. He directed this "power for good" to restore to health the various functions of my body such as my nervous system, digestion, blood condition etc., and to heal all the emotional damage 1 had suffered over the past years. This went on for about ten minutes, during which time I felt unusually relaxed. In fact, I thought I felt a feeling of lightness all over my body. As I left the house I was conscious that Bob's face again looked drained, and his wife was waiting there with another cup of tea.

I had arranged to pay another visit in four days time. Upon my arrival Bob got to work immediately, going through exactly the same procedure as before. This time I felt a tingling sensation throughout my body, and again was aware of the sense of lightness I had experienced on the previous occasion. During the next few days I began to sleep more soundly and my appetite improved.

Most noticeable of all was the change in my attitude to living. No longer did I dash downstairs each morning to read how the Korean War was progressing. Furthermore, it seemed that the world about me was getting lighter. I was emerging from that dark tunnel, and my depression was receding. As the weeks went by I felt that the barrier that had seemed to encircle me had been removed. During my later journeys to Bob's house, some twenty minutes before actually meeting him I would begin to experience the tingling feeling, especially in my hands and feet. This would increase as he dealt with me and continue for some time after I left. It was accompanied by a feeling of inner warmth.

After about eight visits spanning some two months, Bob announced that I was cured. "I can sense nothing more wrong with you," he said. "Don't let your worries get above your collar - if they do, come and see me and I will give you a kick in the pants!" Strange metaphors, I thought. He would accept no payment, insisting that his reward lay in seeing people restored. He said he would lose his gift if he accepted payment.

For months afterwards, whenever I spoke of my experience with Bob, the tingling sensation would return. My spirits were high, my depression gone, and I had a renewed desire to expand my watch repair business. Before long I took up the tenancy of a small workshop in the centre of Bradford from which to provide a service to the jewellery trade.

All continued to go well until I decided to investigate the source of the healing I had received - of which more later.

8

I investigate psychic healing

Following the time that Bob had succeeded in dispelling my depression I repeatedly found myself asking: "How did he do it?" I wondered also how he had been able to restore my vitality and drive. One thing I found curious was that, whenever I related to anyone the story of how Bob had helped me, I would experience again the tingling feeling I had felt when under his ministry. At the same time I wondered how Christianity fitted into all this. There had been an occasion when I had spoken to Bob about Jesus Christ and had asked if he believed that Jesus was the Son of God. His reply had been: "He was a most remarkable, good man, Jack, who did and said some wonderful things, but the universe is so much bigger than that." Obviously, he did not accept the Christian Gospel as the whole truth about God.

At this point in my story I feel it is important to say what I eventually came to believe and know about Bob and his powers. Also, I must explain things about myself that I now know caused me to respond readily to his influence. As a result of this explanation, the reality of the spiritual battle that was to begin in my life at about this time may be easier to discern. Light may be shed on the terrible events that were to take place during the years that followed. I believe that some of my readers may have formed certain conclusions already. For others, the explanation that follows may be unacceptable. It may be especially so for non-Christians. Yet

I would emphasise that for a further fifteen years I too was to find myself quite unable to discern or know what had really been going on in my life.

In a nutshell, Bob was a spiritist. He had mediumistic gifts which he sincerely believed were from God, but which were really counterfeit. The apparently benign spiritual power that worked through him brought with it no message of hope for the soul. Bob taught nothing about Heaven or Hell. He was a perfect example of what the Bible tells us about false signs and wonders to be seen when Satan dresses up as "an angel of light". Never once did he mention God's Holy Spirit, received by those who turn to Christ in real repentance in acknowledgement of mankind's basic sinful nature. The Scriptures speak plainly about what God does when he truly heals us. He delivers us from the powers of darkness and transfers us into the Kingdom of his dear Son. Bob had dispelled the forces of fear but had left me with a greater and more insidious evil spirit, calculated to blind me to the truth about God and Jesus Christ. Hence the tingling feelings I had when testifying about Bob's "healing" gift. When I did attempt to look further into the truth, this power took on a far more sinister form.

You may remember that, as a prisoner of war in Thailand, I had recalled that my mother occasionally had consulted a spiritualist friend about the future. She did have strange dreams that seemed to occur in times of emotional crisis. She was a highly intuitive person, whose premonitions had often come true. Yet as a child she had been baptised into the Christian Church. Later in her life, when she heard I was alive and had been taken prisoner-of-war in Singapore, she had returned to church and had continued to do so up to her death. She was really a confused, not truly "born again" Christian. I now know that, as her son, I had inherited certain of her psychic abilities. The commandment says that the sins of the fathers are visited upon the children of those who hate God (who break his commandments) up to the fourth generation. Unknowingly, my soul was linked to that world of the supernatural against which the Bible warns. It tells that involvement with these things and with all occult practices are abominations to God. Again unknowingly, I had been open to Bob's powers. My poltergeistic and other experiences could be similarly explained.

As I continued to ponder the mystery of how Bob had "healed" me I was troubled with my inability to make it square with what I had heard and learned throughout my years of churchgoing. Then one day, unexpectedly, Agnes's uncle paid us a visit. I had met him only once before, on our wedding day. Somehow he had heard of my depression and the fact that I was now cured. Agnes had told me already that he was a spiritualist, but that she met him only at weddings and funerals. He was very keen to find out just how my problem had been solved. Knowing what I do today about spiritual warfare and the fact that it does not take place in the natural realm, I now wonder very much whether his visit was merely coincidental. For he was to be instrumental in reintroducing darkness into my life.

I told him about my experience with Bob. He appeared not to be interested in the details. Instead, he was quick to tell me that he himself was a healer.

Well," I said, "a few months ago I would have dismissed this sort of thing as poppycock, but now I am at least prepared to hear you out". "Come and see for yourself!", he said. "We meet most weeks at a friend's house". He went on to speak about "spirit guides" and "spirit doctors" who, having supernatural ability and knowledge, were able to direct healing energy directly to where it was needed. I was more sceptical of this idea than I was of Bob's healing "gift". At least, Bob claimed that his gift came from God, and that he was only an agent through whom it worked. Furthermore, he had refused to accept any payment for helping me.

After much persuasion, I agreed to go along and investigate. Really, that was all I wanted to do - carry out a semi-scientific investigation on my own. Today I know that in doing so I had made an extremely foolish and dangerous decision. By deciding to explore this dark territory of spiritism I was stepping outside the bounds of God's grace and breaking God's law. Remember that at this time I was only a church-goer and knew nothing about real Christian doctrine.

Agnes's uncle was called Ronnie. The house in which he and his friends met was only five miles from my. home. It was an old terrace house, with quite large attic rooms that apparently had been used for meetings and seances for thirty years. These people were all psychics whose avowed aim was to contact the departed. I was taken up to the attic, which was bare except for chairs and a small table. Left alone in the place, I was able to sense the presence of a force or power in the room. It had nothing to do with people, because on subsequent occasions, when I explored the attics on my own, I still sensed the presence of this strange energy. Agnes's father accompanied me on these visits, since he too was curious about Ronnie's professed healing powers.

At our first meeting we sat in a loose circle in semi-darkness. A faint red light shone from a lamp in a corner of the room. After a time of quiet, the leader of the group tried to make contact with someone "on the other side". This leader, who owned the house, was a woman of about fifty-five. She had dyed red hair and dark piercing eyes. During this time I listened and looked on with amused curiosity. After several minutes the woman appeared to have gone into some sort of trance. She then started to give messages that purportedly came from a deceased friend of someone present. I recall that the information given was very vague and unspecific. On one occasion during those early weeks Ronnie, supposedly under the control of a departed spirit, began to speak in what appeared to be a foreign language. Afterwards he told me it was Burmese. I firmly contradicted him about this, for whilst I was prisoner-of -war in Burma I had learnt a smattering of the language whist working alongside labourers building the Thailand-Burma railroad. I had spent many months alongside sick and dying Burmese men, and had learned enough to be able to speak to them about their illnesses. In no way could what we heard have been Burmese. Now I realise that it was more likely to have been a Satanic tongue.

The method used by the group to administer healing to one another was to stroke or sweep the hands over affected parts, and this was generally done with a simultaneous expelling of the breath. I do not remember anyone having received instantaneous healing through this treatment. Yet we continued our weekly visits in the hope that we would eventually gain real evidence of physical healing, sufficient to justify Ronnie's claims about himself. Agnes's father had a serious abdominal condition, linked to an injury in World War 1. He had looked forward to receiving some effective ministry for this.

Sadly, round about this time, Agnes's mother was taken seriously ill with a chest infection. Her condition deteriorated rapidly, and having contracted pneumonia, she died of heart failure. She was in her early fifties. After this unexpected event, Agnes spent considerable time alongside her dad. We suspended our visits to Ronnie's meetings.

It was several months later that we received news that the group was to be visited later that year (I think it was 1952) by a very famous medium, a Mrs. Helen Duncan from Glasgow. The fact that this famous person was prepared to visit this comparatively small group made me realise later how deeply involved its members were. This Scots lady had a nation-wide reputation in psychic circles. Middle-aged and heavily built, she spoke with strong Glaswegian accent. I was told that she was an ectoplasmic medium who could summon up the dead and manifest their presence visibly. I had never heard of such a thing before. This, I thought, after it had been explained to me, was too good a chance to miss. Here was an opportunity to discover for certain whether or not there really was an after-life!

Because I was only a churchgoer, a very nominal Christian who had not been truly converted to the faith, I had never entertained any belief in Satan. I had always found embarrassing any mention of him in the scripture readings during church services. Accounts of healing miracles had the same effect upon me. After all, were we not now living in a more enlightened scientific age? The church I attended was somewhat liberal in its theology. Therefore I did not feel guilty about my explorations into the psychic realm. Neither was I aware of the dangers into which this search could lead me.

The meeting was held during one Saturday afternoon in early autumn. Altogether some twenty-five or so people were present. Before anyone was allowed to go upstairs, Mrs. Duncan invited three ladies to accompany her to the attic to examine her clothing. She wore only three items, all black. The attic was bare, except for chairs. One corner of the room had been curtained off with black material, leaving a triangular space just sufficient to conceal Helen Duncan's body. The usual red lamp was positioned nearby. The whole place was carefully searched by myself and others to ensure that no trickery could take place. Eventually we all took our seats and the lights were extinguished. Only the dimly glowing red lamp in the corner remained. We all stayed quiet for some minutes. Then, out of nowhere, we heard a man's voice. It spoke absolutely clearly, and with a refined accent. It was impossible to pinpoint its source. "Is no-one going to speak to me?" it asked. We had been told about Helen Duncan's 'guide', or 'familiar" who was apparently of French origin, by name Albert.

"Souls are gathering around me now" he said, a few minutes later. He went on to describe a young man who had died some years before as a result of a motor-cycle accident. A lady near to me responded immediately. It was a description of her son. Then I saw a white, luminous, ghostly substance proceeding from beneath the curtain behind which Helen Duncan sat. It built up in front at us to form the figure of a blond-haired young man, his every feature clearly defined. I remember particularly his fingernails and every detail of his hand! Then information about the circumstances of the accident wore given that were apparently unknown at the time. I think this was given by Albert, and not by the apparition. All this happened long before the time of writing and I am not certain about that one fact. About everything else I am quite certain. Several so-called "departed souls" appeared before us, each known to

76

someone present. One such was a young woman carrying a baby in her arms. Her name was given as Alice, and the story told to us of how she had died following the birth at the child. Apparently her kidneys had failed. I knew that my mother had a younger sister called Alice who had died in childbirth, but I did not know the cause of death. Later I asked my mother what had happened. "Her kidneys closed", she said simply. This was an expression commonly used by lay people in those days to describe kidney failure.

After those appearances had been going on for a while I decided to take a closer look at one of the figures. These manifestations had been taking place right in front of me, some four feet from where I was sitting, which was on the front row. Suddenly, I stood up and momentarily put my head "inside" the apparition. I remember experiencing a smell of onions - perhaps it was not quite the same as onions and this very pronounced odour remained with me for some time afterwards. Furthermore, I developed a sore throat and lost my voice for a few hours. Obviously there had been some sort of energy at work.

After an hour or so the electoplasmic appearances became weaker, and the session was then closed. When Helen Duncan emerged from behind the curtain, she appeared to be very, very tired. When the curtain was drawn back we saw only the chair on which she had been sitting. Apparently the purpose of the curtain was to prevent us from seeing what would have been the bizarre spectacle of ectoplasm emerging from her various natural orifices whilst she was in a trance.

Many years later, whilst browsing through the city library, I read in a book somewhere that Helen Duncan had died following a police raid on a house in which she was operating. Knowing what I know now, if on that occasion she had been in a trance and had been "out of the body" then the shock of such a violent intrusion would have killed her. What I found surprising was the fact that the writer had then attempted to discredit her completely, saying that rolls of mutton cloth and the like had been found nearby and that these materials had been used to trick those who had presumably paid to come to the meeting.

All I can say is that everything I have recorded above is absolutely true. Non-spiritual, completely materialistic people will never be able to accept any happening, evil or benign, that is claimed to be supernatural in origin. Even within the Church this is so. Christians of a certain persuasion insist that the miracles performed by Christ were signs and wonders intended to prove only to the first-century Church that he really was the Son of God. They maintain that such things do not happen today. For now, they point out, we have the Bible, in which we find all we need to receive salvation of our souls and wholeness of being. Sadly, what I have just written about these people used to describe me exactly!

I now know that Christians who accept such a doctrine are like ostriches with their heads in the sand. This I hope to make clear as I record the extent to which I came under attack from Satan. For I was to experience the reality of magical powers and occultism in all its forms. I was to fall prey to the Evil One's deceptive and seductive forces, that exist to entrap and destroy those who love God. Fortunately for me, I was also to experience the reality of God's protection as part of his plan for me. Above all, I was to come to know with utter certainty the authority of Christ over all that is evil.

9

Darkness returns and accidents happen

By this time I was so busy with watch-glass work and watch repairs that I would have done well to have concentrated on nothing else. However, I had been so intrigued by what I had seen on the day of Helen Duncan's visit that I wanted to find out more. My regular attendances at church were a constant reminder to me that I had not succeeded in finding out whether Bob's power had really been from God or if it was compatible with Christianity. Neither had I been convinced of the validity of uncle Ronnie's claims. I began to attend the weekly meetings again.

One evening Ronnie suggested we do things differently. He asked the group to sit in a circle. Then he requested that we join hands and empty our minds. At that point I felt a terrific thump in my solar plexus. I became very troubled emotionally and during the days following I found myself slipping back into depression. I became preoccupied with the investigation of psychic phenomena and the supernatural. I began to visit the city library and to take out every book available there on the subject. Soon I was in the very pit of depression.

In St. Matthew's Gospel, Chapter 12, at verse 43, Jesus tells us: "When an evil spirit comes out of a man, it goes through arid places seeking rest and does not find it. Then it says, 'I will return to the house I left'. When it arrives it finds the house unoccupied, swept clean and put in order. Then it goes and takes with it seven other spirits more wicked than itself, and they go in and live there. And the final condition of that man is worse than the first". (New International Version of the Bible)

Looking back, many years later, I realised that I had been in the same position as the man Jesus was talking about. Bob, with his benign but counterfeit powers, had dealt with my spiritual problems and had appeared to have driven out the darkness. Yet he had not led me to Christ, so that God's promised Holy Spirit might indwell me. Instead, he had left within me the counterfeit "consistent with all that is good" spirit he had spoken of. When, at that evening meeting, I had agreed to join hands with Ronnie and his friends, I had linked myself directly with them. As I had emptied my mind and ceased to exert my will, I had opened myself up to even more evil spiritual forces.

After that, my father-in-law and I stopped going to the spiritist meetings Although I was able to pursue my business quite normally, underneath it all was darkness and confusion of spirit. In the midst of all this, as I was walking down a city street one day, a verse of Scripture came to my mind. It was a well-known verse from Isaiah that I had no doubt heard many times since childhood without its ever having meant much to me. It was from Isaiah Chapter 40, at verse 31. which promises that "those who hope in the Lord will renew their strength. They will soar on wings like eagles; they will run and not grow weary, they will walk and not be faint". (N.l.V.) For a few moments my spirit had lifted and I was momentarily brought into the light.

At work my thoughts turned to diversification, and I began to experiment with the production of watch glasses, using the then fairly new material, Perspex acrylic sheet. It was not long before I had developed a viable means of manufacture and was able to produce the popular sizes. There was a very real demand for them from the trade and I soon found it necessary to employ three part-time assistants. At the beginning of 1952 our son David had been born. In early 1954 Agnes had become pregnant again and now we had to think of moving house. We eventually moved into a fairly old terrace house. It stood in a reasonably respectable area about a mile away from our church. During the years we lived there we were never very happy. Our second son, Philip, was born in December, by which time Agnes had been diagnosed as suffering from a heart condition known as mitral stenosis. This causes breathlessness, due to the tissue of the mitral valve having hardened, with the result that an inadequate supply of blood is pumped around the body. This condition was to worsen quite rapidly during the next few years. Up to this time we had been unable to afford private transport and I had travelled to and from work by bus. Now business was brisk and our financial position had eased. We decided to take the plunge and buy a car. We found a Ford Popular model that was just a few years old and of good appearance. To help pay for it I generally worked from late evening into the early hours of the following day. At weekends we drove out into the country, and this helped to lift my depression, which still hung over me like a dark shadow. The amazing thing was that my energy and drive had not been affected. I still attended church regularly but remained spiritually confused. I seemed to lack control over my thought life, particularly when I was not busy concentrating on my job. Unclean thoughts began to enter my consciousness, and various temptations kept coming my way. I found that there was a conflict going on inside me. Something was trying to persuade me that nothing really mattered and therefore it was all right to give way to temptation, yet deep in my inner self I knew that these thoughts were untrue, and this gave me the power to resist.

One Saturday in the summer of 1957 we decided to head for the Trough of Bowland in Lancashire, a beauty spot that neither Agnes or I had ever visited. The weather was sunny, with the promise of only the occasional shower. We set off soon after lunch, and took a picnic with us. By mid-afternoon we were well on the way to our destination when we ran into a heavy downpour. We decided to stop in a lay-by and have an early picnic tea. The rain eventually stopped, and we set off again on our journey. Soon we arrived at the top of a hill. It was of medium gradient, and the road was wide and had a smooth, tarmac surface. On either side were modern houses, and between the pavement and the road was a grassed area about six feet wide, in which young trees had been planted every twenty yards. The rain that had fallen earlier was evaporating in the sunshine, and I suppose it had reached that critical point at which the road surface had become slippery through a mixture of dampness, oil and dirt. We were about fifty yards down the hill when the back end of the car started to swing from side to side. I tried to correct the steering, but to no avail. In seconds, the car was spinning down the hill like a top. Gradually, the road camber steered it towards the left and, a couple of hundred yards further down, it mounted the curb and hit one of the young trees. The car struck it broadside on and almost exactly in the middle, virtually folding the vehicle in two. David, our older son, had been standing up in the back of the car. The rear window had shattered into countless pieces, many of which had struck his head and face. The glass had not been of the laminated type used in modern vehicles. Philip, being only three years old, had remained sitting down, and was hardly touched. Margaret and Agnes had also escaped injury. None of us had suffered broken bones. David, on the other hand, had been badly injured around the eyes and head, and was covered in blood. I snatched him out of the car and ran up the road with him in my arms, shouting out in great distress. I remember thinking that if David's sight were gone and if his face were unrecognisable I would rather he were dead.

Someone must have telephoned for help, and an ambulance soon arrived. We were all taken to the nearest hospital and detained overnight. Next day, leaving David behind, Agnes, Margaret, Philip and I left for home by train. For the next ten days, friends drove us to the hospital and back each day. Our car had been a write-off. Then David's stitches - some forty in all - were removed, and he was allowed home. Over the next year he received extensive plastic surgery, and was left with only minimal scarring. I believe now that this incident was not without significance in our spiritual battle. For, twenty years later, David was to be ordained into the priesthood of the Anglican Church.

I have met those whose understanding and experience of life has always been purely material. Whilst perhaps admitting to being agnostic, they dismiss completely the whole idea of Satan's existence. Any belief that if we allowed ourselves to come under his power he could ever control our destiny they consider to be absolute rubbish.

Most inhabitants of the western world will surely take this view. It is logical for them to do so because their reasoning is based on natural law. To allow Satan to have control over us and to have any concept either of him or the reality of good and evil, our souls must first become linked to the supernatural realm. We can seek deliberately to do this, as do all those who want to contact the dead, or who actually believe in Satan and seek to be involved in his occult activities. This realm of the supernatural is what St. Paul meant by "the heavenly realms" when he explained in his letter to the Ephesian church (Chapter 6), the nature of spiritual warfare, the reality of which he himself had no doubt. The "born again", mature Christian, who allows only God's Holy Spirit to control his life, has the whole armour of God at his disposal, as St. Paul went on to point out.

I had not deliberately sought to be on the side of evil. I thought I had set out to discover the truth about Bob and Christ. Yet by the route I have described I had come under the influence of Satan and his demonic powers. That he had the ability and right to influence our minds and actions and lead us down wrong paths I did not know then to be true. By the Holy Spirit the Christian is promised guidance and protection, together with all other blessings of the Christian life, if he walks closely with God. Those who have unwittingly stepped out of the bounds of God's grace to explore the supernatural realm are in danger of being picked off by Satan, whose ultimate aim is to destroy us. Fortunately, God knows those who truly love him. By his grace, he is prepared to reach out into the depths of darkness to rescue and deliver us. Unfortunately for me, worse things were to happen before such deliverance could come.

10

The "Get Ahead" Competition

We gradually recovered from the shock of the accident, and early in 1958 we bought another car. It was a black Morris Oxford, large and comfortable, and ideal for taking our parents around the Yorkshire Dales.

One day early in the summer, Agnes noticed an announcement in Radio Times. It concerned a competition to be held on a live outside-broadcast television programme, to be called The B.B.C. "Get Ahead" Competition. Applications were invited from people who considered they were developing a business that had unique possibilities but where an injection of cash was needed. The competition was to be run in conjunction with the "News Chronicle", a national daily that was struggling to survive. Agnes persuaded me to apply. On a single sheet of A4 I typed a glowing outline of my watch-glass manufacturing business. I received a reply by return, and was asked to attend for interview at the Russell Hotel, London, where I would stay overnight. I seemed to receive special attention as soon as I arrived. Without wasting much time the gentleman in charge whisked me into a private room, where I was interviewed by himself and two others. After the interview I was told that the live broadcasts would come from a large hall in Maida Vale. The competitors would be accommodated in a hotel nearby, and I was told that I had been chosen to take part in the first heat. Sixteen competitors were to be chosen out of five thousand applicants. There were to be four heats and a final, to be held over five weeks. It was not long before I received a first class return ticket to London, together with details of accommodation booked at a first class hotel. I was required to be there by early morning on the day of the broadcast. It was necessary to have a "dry run" on the set, and there was to be a private interview with the V.l.P.s who were to question the first four competitors that night. I was quite fearful about having to appear live before ten million viewers, and I found out later that the producer also was worried that I might not be able to cope. What he and his team were actually looking for was good programme material. Apparently this thirty-nine year-old, rather intense Yorkshireman, former Japanese prisoner-of-war turned watch-glass manufacturer, was just the sort of person they had in mind. That is, if he could cope with the stress involved. For I was to be the first to speak, announcing my name and home town and what my business was about.

I had not seen Bob since I had agreed to let him help me with my depression some years before. Now I felt an inner prompting to visit him. By this time he had moved further up the Aire valley into a modern house on the daleside, and had built onto it a special extension - a room reserved especially for seeing clients. I told him of my fears about the competition. which was due to take place in a fortnight "Don't worry at all," he said. "It will be quite all right on the night. I will be watching, and in control."

The day of the competition arrived. The four of us did our dry run, and had our private interview with the panel of V.l.Ps. during the afternoon. As the time of the programme approached I grew more and more tense, and my mouth became dry. Four cubicles of transparent plastic had been erected side by side, with the name of a competitor above each one, and we were asked to stand in these. They had been placed in alphabetical order, so that I was first on the left. Before the programme started the cubicles and the hall were in complete darkness. Then silence was called for. After a while we heard, from a speaker somewhere out of sight, the voice of an announcer telling of a programme to be put out later in the evening. He continued: "And now." - at which point another voice began the count-down to the start of our programme - "Ten, nine, eight.. ." It was just then that a powerful feeling gripped my solar plexus. It took away all emotion, and all fear and all trembling left my body. It was at the exact spot at which I had felt the 'thump' when I had foolishly joined hands with Ronnie and his friends on that fatal evening a few years before.

Suddenly, my cubicle was flooded with light. Then, on the count of zero, I found myself announcing quite clearly to ten million viewers, "My name is John Butterfield. I live in Shipley, West Yorkshire, and I manufacture watchglasses."

The programme, and the competition, had begun. After my three co-competitors had announced themselves, we were then called individually to another part of the set to face our interviewers. I, of course, was the first to be called. Once the questioning had begun, all trace of nervousness left me. The programme was introduced on this first occasion by Kenneth Horne, a well-known show-business personality of the day. I received a high score in answer to my questions, and at the end of the contest I found I had won the heat. The final camera shot was of myself receiving the heat-winner's cheque for one hundred and odd pounds. We then went across to the hotel for drinks.

When I retired to bed I pondered about the evening. I was amazed by what had happened at the start of the programme. That Bob had strange powers was now without doubt, and it had been proved that he could use them at a distance. Yet I was unable to see then that they were from an evil source. Perhaps I believed they were neutral. Also, I felt convinced that it had been contrived that I should win the heat. The programme was hosted the following week by Peter West, another well-known T.V. personality. Kenneth Horne had been taken ill with heart trouble and was in hospital. At the hotel, no expense had been spared. The food and accommodation were of the highest order. The whole thing was becoming very exciting, both for myself and my friends, who all said they were "rooting" for me. After only one appearance I was recognised by people everywhere I went! This especially seemed to happen in the London Underground. I was quite surprised to win the second heat, because there had been some really excellent competition. However, I was delighted to collect another cheque.

Among the celebrities who had questioned us was a politician, a trade union leader, and a leading industrialist. I also met Barbara Cartland, the romantic novelist, with whom I and others shared afternoon tea. Both she her daughter, the then Lady Lewisham, acted as judges on separate occasions.

In the end, I won my way to the final. I took third place, having won a total of seven hundred pounds in all. The first prize was given to a man of about my own age who I am sure was a far better business man than I was. He had invented a collapsible electric clothes-drier. It was ingenious, but certainly was no threat to big business. I was told by a trade friend in London that my competitors in Clerkenwell had breathed a sigh of relief when they heard I had not won the competition. I settled down to work again and decided to spend my winnings researching the development of an automatic press for producing wrist-watch glasses. I was introduced by a friend to a small. firm of engineers and was impressed with their ideas and keen interest in my project.

The fact that I had not won the competition outright had not depressed me at all. I had been in no position to expand immediately, because I had no means of mass-production. I needed to make tools and machines to do the job. The deep depression that I had known during the previous years had lifted somewhat during the excitement of the competition, but now the darkness began to return. Again, uncleanness and temptations started to invade my thoughts. Although I pressed on with my work, this brought no let-up to the confusion and depression that continued to marr my life.

Summer and autumn passed, and I began to look forward to Christmas. Surely, I thought, this would be a time when, surrounded by my wife and family and by so many loving friends at church, I would be able to find happiness.

I was to have no warning of the impending tragedy through which God would shortly intervene in my life.

11

Disaster strikes, and I cry out to God

It was about ten o'clock on Tuesday, 22nd December, 1958, when I left my business premises and made for home. For some days the weather had been cold, murky and unpleasant, and drizzle was falling steadily through the watery mist that was present everywhere.

I had arranged with Agnes that I would bring fish and chips home for supper. As I approached our usual shop I saw that its lights were out, and then remembered that it did not open on Tuesdays. I negotiated the nearby roundabout and took a different direction. I knew there were a couple of shops on the road to the next town. The night was still filthy, and I drove with caution. I was pleased to find that the second shop, which was on the right hand side of the road, was still open and empty of customers. I parked the car and dashed quickly across. I was served immediately.

Back in the car, I decided I had better not execute a U-turn. Instead, I decided to drive into the street adjacent to the shop and turn round there. I checked in my rear mirror, saw all was clear, then indicated right and turned slowly across the road. I had almost reached the other side when I experienced a terrific impact against the offside of my car. It was at a point just in front of me, and the heavy vehicle swung round through several degrees. The quietness that had prevailed hitherto was now shattered by the high-pitched, continuous, loud roar of a motor-cycle engine. The machine, riderless and upturned, lay some thirty or forty yards down the road. Its driver had been killed instantly, the pillion passenger terribly injured.

The next few days seemed like a nightmare that ceased only when we slept, only to recommence each morning when we awoke. We learned that the inquest would be delayed for months until the pillion passenger had fully recovered. Both he and the driver had been young men aged about twenty. No witnesses had come forward, and the police had warned me of possible prosecution. I have only vague memories of that Christmas. With this terrible burden hanging over us, every day seemed endless. At work some weeks later a close friend called to see me. It was late afternoon, and he had bought a copy of the local evening newspaper. Its front page headlines jumped out at me.

The wife of the dead man, expecting their baby, had taken her own life.

Without speaking, my friend left. Alone in my workshop, already desperate with worry, the shock of this news was more than I could take. Suddenly I seemed to be standing outside myself, looking on at my life. I could see the mess, the spiritual confusion, the unclean desires, the utter hypocrisy of my churchgoing. It was then that I believe God drew near to me. I was aware of an awesome holiness, and was brought to my knees. I cried out in words I cannot remember. I know I was broken and repentant, unable to take any more mental anguish. I pleaded to God to have mercy on me.

As I locked up my premises and made for home, I realised that I now had peace in my heart. It was a strange feeling, for it was purely an emotional peace. An inner quietness had come over me, and I realised that the fear, the confusion, the uncleanness, and above all, the darkness that had entered my soul at that spiritist meeting years before had been instantly dispelled. Yet, as I set off to catch the bus, my mind still carried the terrible burden of worry.

I had got about half way home - I can still recall vividly the exact spot - when I heard a faint, inner voice speak to me. It was if it had spoken into my right ear, yet I heard it not through my ear's physical mechanism, but deep inside my head.

"Don't worry," it said. "it's all part of the plan."

That was all, but I knew it was true and that it was from God - because peace had come to my mind also.

For some time after that I was given a strange insight, almost a revelation to my inner mind, that assured me that nothing that ever happens is accidental. Today I find that proposition intellectually quite unacceptable - the revelation is no longer real. Yet I once heard on the radio a similar pronouncement by a man who had passed through a traumatic, near-death experience and had miraculously emerged alive. During that time, he said, he had been conscious that every event in our lives fitted into a giant divine pattern.

A similar story was related to me some time ago by someone who was a good friend for many years prior to his death. A highly spiritual man, he was a senior probation officer whose work brought him into contact with murderers and psychopaths in some of Britain's high security prisons. He lived close to God, that he might keep his peace and retain his inner strength. During a summer holiday in France he had a massive heart attack, and whilst on the operating table his heart actually stopped beating for some two minutes. He told me that during that time he seemed to be in a new dimension of consciousness, and had become aware of a mind all around him that was infinitely great and all-knowing - an experience he could not adequately describe to me. Surely, I thought, he is describing the mind of God! The experiences of these two people, although subjective like mine, helped to confirm to me what the Bible says about God's omniscience, omnipresence and absolute wisdom. For such is the nature of God's Spirit of Truth, promised to us through faith in Jesus Christ.

Following this experience, a great inner peace which was almost a feeling of joy came upon Agnes and myself as we endeavoured to live one day at a time. I remember that people would ask us how we managed to get through these days without sinking into deep depression. Something had happened within our inner beings that had showed us that contentment and happiness in life does not depend on externals such as wealth or even freedom from physical disability. Rather, in practice, it depended on having inner strength, upliftment of spirit and the sort of mental attitude that somehow was being given to us at that time. I believe now that this was the Holy Spirit at work in us. He made us secure in the knowledge that God loves each one of us individually.

Two months later, quite unexpectedly, a young couple who had witnessed the accident contacted the police. It transpired that before this time they had felt too scared to come forward. Then, some six months after the accident, the inquest was held. After hearing all the evidence, a verdict of "death by misadventure" was recorded.

It had taken several months to repair the car, and when I first drove again I did so with great apprehension. Yet it was not long before I sensed that I was being protected and guided away from danger. I had strange evidences of this, details of which would take too long to relate. The world around me was no longer dark, but as yet I was not a Christian. For at no time had I ever really been challenged personally to trust my life to Christ, neither had the true meaning of the Gospel ever been brought home to me. Yet a change had taken place deep within myself. In theological terms God had delivered my soul from the power of darkness that had been at work within me; I had yet to be transferred into the kingdom of his dear Son. Such is one Biblical description of what salvation is about. (Colossians Ch.1, v.13) Occasions still arose when I was tempted as before. Now, however, I would get on my knees before God, and in no time at all I would be presented with a way of escape. It seemed that this God who had come to me when on my knees before him in my attic workshop really did hear me when I prayed from my heart.

12

Good things happen: I become a Christian

During the winter of 1959-60 Agnes contracted severe bronchitis followed by an attack of "Asian Flu". Her heart began to fail, and I became aware of a squeaking sound that accompanied each rapid heartbeat. She had developed epicarditis - inflammation of the sac that surrounds the heart. I called in our doctor very late one night, and she was admitted to hospital immediately. I pleaded with the doctor that the possibility of surgery might be investigated. After some weeks in hospital the infection had been overcome., and Agnes had regained strength Then one day the senior heart surgeon appeared at her bedside.

"After studying X-Rays some days ago I thought there was nothing we could do for you", he said. "but now we think you have a fifty-fifty chance of pulling through. What do you feel about that?".

Agnes later described what happened to her then. "I felt to be bathed in light, and then I heard a voice, a clear, happy voice, which said: 'Now what are you going to do? Are you going to trust me?' Immediately I replied, 'Yes, please'."

The lady in the next bed told us that the surgeon had barely asked the question before Agnes had responded. The operation was carried out just over a week later. In those days, all that could be done for Agnes's heart condition was to open up the damaged heart valve. To do this involved removing a rib in order to gain access, from the back, to the still beating heart.

When 1 visited Agnes next day she resembled a corpse. I remember that, on seeing her, I broke down and wept. Yet not only was she alive, but she began to make such rapid progress that within a week all sign of shock had gone. She was then sent to a hospital at Ilkley in the Yorkshire Dales to begin six weeks of recuperation.

During that time we sold the house and bought a brand new one three miles further down the valley. Margaret, then thirteen years old, worked all hours with me to clear out our old abode and decorate our new house. It was a three-bedroomed semi-detached, with open-plan gardens, a large kitchen and a sizable through lounge. On her discharge from hospital, still a little weak but otherwise in good health, Agnes received a lovely surprise.

Towards the end of 1960 I moved my business into new premises. An acquaintance of mine had told me there were vacant ground-floor rooms in an old textile mill just on the edge of the city. I had decided that they would suit my purposes at least temporarily. By this time I had accumulated a fair amount of heavy machinery, including two heavy presses and a large lathe. We had several steel stock shelves and needed an inspection and packing area.

As I look back to that time, I realise that my spiritual life had still not been. sorted out. I had retained a sense of gratitude to Bob and some allegiance to him, and on one occasion sought his help again. Shortly after completing the work on the garage and garden paths I developed a severe, persistent ache in my lower back. After many weeks it had shown no sign of improvement, and I decided to ask Bob for help. The pain disappeared after paying him just a few visits. It was as if I had received a new supply of nervous energy, and I suppose I still remained puzzled as to its true source. However, puzzled or not, I was free of pain, still not depressed, and concerned merely to live a normal life. I certainly had no intention of investigating psychic matters further, though I now realise that I was still well-and-truly linked to the supernatural realm in which those forces operate. For I had made no renunciation of them, and I still had faith in Bob and his powers. The difference, however, was that I had come to believe that God really existed, and that he was holy and all-knowing - a fearful, supreme power to be reckoned with.

Fortunately for me, the most important time of my life was rapidly approaching.

In 1964, the man who had been vicar of my church for eight years decided to move on. After many months of waiting we learned that a new, younger man had been appointed to our parish. Shortly afterwards he was inducted and installed in office.

Our new vicar, the Rev. Brandon D. Jackson, had been trained at a theological college which had a strong Conservative Evangelical tradition. To him the Bible really was the word of God, and he had a great love of the Christian Gospel. Brandon had been soundly converted as a young man, following the loss of a close relative. He was quick to discern whether or not a person was a true Christian. In my capacity as Secretary to the Parochial Church Council, Brandon and I met frequently to discuss parish business. It was after he had been alongside me for about eighteen months, that he said to me one day:

"Jack, you're not really a Christian. Your heart is in the right place, but you need sorting out."

This statement, coming suddenly out of the blue, really shook me. I had been a churchgoer since childhood and a choir member for thirty years, and was now Secretary of The P.C.C. - furthermore, I was fifteen years older than he was! After considerable argument, I agreed to challenge him on a formal basis by attending his weekly study group. I would jolly well show him who needed sorting out!

Brandon held his Bible study group at the vicarage on Wednesday evenings. Some thirty people attended it, and it was with considerable difficulty that everyone managed to squeeze into the lounge. Fortunately, it was a large room. Brandon would usually perch on a small table in one corner, from which position he had an overview of all present. I soon realised why the meetings were so well attended. Brandon may not have been "Charismatic" in spirituality, but he certainly had a charismatic personality. Furthermore, he was able to expound the Scriptures very clearly and convincingly. I found him most interesting and amusing. After a month or two I began to realise that never before had I been truly challenged by the Gospel. Never before had anyone said that I needed to let Jesus, who was truly alive in the spiritual sense, take charge of my life. At last I began to make sense of the doctrine of the atonement, and to recognise the central claim of the Gospel - that Jesus died for my sins, and rose again to bring new life to me. Yet I found it difficult to accept the truth of this. I kept thinking about Bob and what he had said about "the power consistent with all that is good in the world." Then I hit upon a real snag. We had reached the Gospel passage where Jesus cast out the money-changers from the temple in Jerusalem. It described how Jesus had made himself a whip of cords for this purpose (John Ch.2 V.15). At this point I found myself saying something like: "Surely that can't be right! Jesus wouldn't do a thing like that!"

The spirit of "all that is good in the world" of which Bob had spoken had convinced me that the use any sort of violence by Jesus to achieve his ends could not be consistent with his divine nature. How subtle Satan is'! Nowhere in the Bible do we see any reference to a spirit of "all that is good in the world". The Spirit of God is the Holy Spirit of Truth.

My outburst brought the study to a standstill. I was greatly upset and unable to think straight. Brandon left the room and returned with a book which he asked me to take away and read. When I returned home that evening I was emotionally very upset. There was no way I could settle down to read the book. I went to bed and decided to give the matter to God.

Early next morning I had what I can only describe as a waking dream. In this dream I was standing in the temple in Jerusalem. I knew I was at the place where Jesus had been when he drove out the money-changers. Strangely, I did not see the building, or people. or anything at all. Then it was that Jesus spoke to me. "Jack," he said, "evil has to be either in or out, there is no half-way place. So it has to be with you also."

I remember waking up knowing that I had heard the truth, and that I had been set free from the false belief I had been deceived into accepting. Quickly, I sought out Brandon and told him of my experience. He accepted what I told him. I was able to rejoin the study group with a new spirit of excitement, eager to learn more of the deep Gospel truths that were unfolding under Brandon's teaching He seemed to discern the stage each of us had reached in our spiritual walk, and would ask questions of us unexpectedly. I remember my heart pounding when I thought he was going to pounce on me! Then after about six months I found I was able occasionally to join in the prayers at the end of the study. My heart would be in my mouth before I spoke, such was the apprehension and self-consciousness I felt. Yet something within me seemed to impel me to pray. I am sure many people are able to identify with how I felt on those occasions.

One day I realised that I had come to understand and believe the Christian Gospel. Yet Brandon constantly was at pains to point out to us that to become Christians it would be necessary to ask Jesus Christ into our lives, and so have a relationship with God through him. He had spelt out to us at length the doctrines of justification by faith and of the atonement. He had stressed the necessity of true repentance in order to receive God's forgiveness - something he said could come only by recognising our basic sinful nature as part of a fallen creation. As an Evangelical Christian, Brandon's faith was centred on Christ's work of redemption on the Cross. I found out later that when Brandon left theological college he already had the reputation of being a "hell-fire" preacher! As he taught the Christian faith from the Bible, in no way did he intend to compromise the Gospel. Before he preached the Good News, he was careful to spell out the bad news - that eternity would be spent either in Heaven or Hell! We would need to acknowledge that we could not help ourselves, and decide to give our lives to Jesus

Christ. If we did this, he said, we would become "children of God" and receive the promised Holy Spirit, who would direct our lives and lead us into all truth. Brandon pointed out that, in the end, each one of us had to make a choice; our conversion would depend on an act of will. Indeed, if we did make a decision for Christ we might not feel any different, but we should believe that the promise of eternal life is true, and know that faith does not depend on feelings.

So I made that commitment. It was not accompanied by emotion; there were no tears, or feelings of great joy. Thereafter I would ask Brandon at regular intervals whether or not I really was a Christian. His reply was always the same. "If you have a personal relationship with Jesus Christ, Jack, then you are a Christian". I wondered whether I had such a relationship. I would listen to various people praying at Church, and some of them seemed to talk to God as if they were on really close terms with him. They called him "Father", and appeared genuinely thankful to him for sending his son Jesus, with whom they seemed to have an even closer relationship. As the weeks went by I grew more and more frustrated and envious.

It was on the following Easter Saturday (I was forty-seven and the year was 1965) that I asked Brandon for the last time whether or not I was truly a Christian. I had taken some flowers to church that afternoon, to be used for decorating the building for Easter Day. When I received the usual answer I looked up to heaven with a frustrated, intense longing I shall never forget. Silently, from my heart, I shouted "If there's something more, for heaven's sake let me know!"

Little did expect what happened next! When I awoke next morning I seemed to be walking on air! There was a joy in my heart such as I had never experienced before. Moreover, the person of Jesus and what he had done for me had become real. When I read my Bible, I found that words I had previously read many times had now become alive, revealing truths I had never recognised before. Now I knew the reality of the promise found at the beginning of St. John's Gospel that those who believe in the name of Jesus would be given the right and the power to become children of God! I saw that "believing in his name" really meant knowing exactly who Jesus was and is. I could now believe that, when on earth, he was "God with us", and that, as the risen Christ, he now reigns for eternity with God in heaven. I found this revelation truly mind-blowing. As a child of God, the Bible promised me a multitude of things, every one of them positive and for my benefit. I would receive every spiritual blessing in Jesus Christ. With him as my Lord, I could gradually be changed into his likeness through the Spirit at work within me. The Bible said I had access to God's power - the same power that raised Jesus from the dead. It promised protection and guidance so long as I stayed within the bounds of God's grace. This Jesus, who loved me with a never-ending love, would present me blameless before God his Father when he returned to judge the world. All these things, and many more, could be mine. To try to take it all in was truly beyond me. However, for the very first time, I knew the joy of my salvation.

When I returned to work after Easter that joy was still with me. I remember that as I looked out of the factory window onto the busy street below I had a longing to tell the passers-by about Jesus.

I came to realise that I had undergone a Holy Spirit experience, such as St. Paul had prayed for in his letter to the Ephesian Church. Here he had asked that they receive a spirit of wisdom and revelation in the knowledge of God, so that, having their spiritual eyes opened, they would know the hope of his calling and his immeasurable power available to Christian believers.

I was unaware at first of what had happened to me, and knew nothing about the gifts of the Holy Spirit. I did not know that when Christians have experiences of the Spirit that they sometimes receive the gift of tongues, for example. This did not happen to me, but something did happen which showed me that God's Kingdom is a supernatural one in which extraordinary events take place such as were the norm in New Testament times. Shortly after Easter there was to be a special meeting of the Church Council at which we were to make an important decision concerning the rebuilding of the church halls. Brandon always opened Council meetings by reading a portion of Scripture, followed by prayers. The day before the meeting I found that I was aware, in some remarkable way, of the verses Brandon would read to us. When I told Agnes about this she suggested I type them out, with an explanatory note about what had happened. I did this, and before the meeting I said to Brandon: "You may soon need to open this, or you may not."

Brandon had brought along his large, family Bible for this special occasion. A strange thrill went through me when he read out the exact verses the Holy Spirit had given to me. They were from the Book of Nehemiah, and were to do with the rebuilding of the walls of Jerusalem. When he had taken his seat again I invited him to open the envelope. He had a most perplexed look as he handed the note to his wife! I often wonder whether they ever came to understand what had really happened. I came to see that I had received a "word of knowledge". There was an equally remarkable sequel to Brandon's challenge to the church. In order to rebuild our Sunday Schools we needed to find what would be a quarter of a million pounds by today's values. Never once had he asked us directly for money, but for many weeks had preached about spiritual rebuilding. After a week of prayer, church members were asked to pledge the amount they felt it was right for them to give. We completed a slip which we put on the offertory plate on the following Sunday. After the evening service, the Vicar, Treasurer and Churchwardens met in the vicarage to work out the total amount promised. Over three hundred slips had been handed in. It was quite late by the time the total had been arrived at - fifty pounds short of the target figure. Then there was a clatter as an envelope dropped through the letter box.

In it were ten five pound notes.

13

God intervenes in my business

Our business continued to grow steadily, and in 1965 I succeeded in semi-automating the production process for watch-glass manufacture. This almost doubled our production capacity. I had virtually only just completed the machines when we were offered the entire business of the largest outlet in the U.K. This put us on a sound financial footing, and we decided to accept an offer from the local authority to erect for us a purpose-built factory not many miles from home. We were given a twenty-one year lease on the property. It was exciting to watch the new building take shape before our eyes. We moved into our new factory in October 1968.

In those early days after our move I was conscious of an unseen presence with me that kept me at peace in what could have been a fearful time.

A parking space for cars had been provided across the full length of our building. Its boundary, separating our premises from a main road, was defined by a new low wall. During the previous ten years this whole district had been demolished and rebuilt, and was unrecognisable as the same area as before. It was many years later that I suddenly realised that the entrance to our building exactly overlooked the spot where, on that dark December night in 1958, that fatal motor-cycle accident had happened.

When, those years later, we did eventually realise that on every visit to work we had passed the site of that dreadful accident, we realised also that a remarkable thing had happened. For not only had God hidden from us until then the memory of that terrible event, but he had healed our mind and spirit from its effects, and had taken away its power to hurt us. Throughout the time we worked in that factory - some fourteen years - not once did we undergo any emotional trauma as a result of that awful experience. The possibility of such complete healing is often denied by secular counsellors and psychotherapists, who state with negative assurance that the emotional scars will remain for life. Yet I had been shown that if we truly seek God's mercy and forgiveness he is able to lead us out of the deepest darkness and provide a new beginning.

Such knowledge and wisdom was not yet ours as we continued our business life in our brand new premises. The work was hard, and we had borrowed money from the bank to finance new equipment and stock of raw materials. We had found a Swiss firm that specialised in the production of watch-glass quality acrylic sheet in a variety of thicknesses. We were invited to look round their factory, and were offered yearly contracts at prices at least thirty per cent below those of any British or other foreign manufacturer. We were only too glad to accept these terms. Such low prices were to prove a vital factor in our struggle to make a profit in the face of increasing competition from abroad.

Just over a year after moving into our new premises, orders from the large distributor of watch parts began to fall off considerably. It turned out that the managing director had believed a rumour that we had collaborated with our main competitor to fix prices. Instead of confronting me with this, our customer had transferred part of his business to a French firm for a price fractionally lower than ours, and had signed a contract with them. Actually, the meeting we had with our competitor, arranged at his request, was to discuss how we might deal with high pressure competition from a Dutch manufacturer who was trying desperately to break into the U.K. market.

This substantial loss of business meant that, unless steps were taken quickly to redress the balance, we would be in serious trouble. 'And just what', I thought, 'does God think he is doing?

What about all those promises of guidance and protection?' I started to feel quite annoyed and depressed. Nevertheless, I decided one lunchtime to go into church and spend time working out what to do. Once inside the church, I made my way to the communion rail. I knelt down and began to pray to God. "Father", I said, "get me out of this mess and I'll do anything for you, anything at all".

I know now that to pray such a prayer is a very dangerous thing to do! When God knows we really mean business with him, he is liable to take us seriously. Yet I believe that God, who knows what is in our hearts, had led me to plead with him and make that promise.

Very shortly after that time, John, who was my main London watch-glass distributor, came up from London with his wife to spend a weekend with us. I had first met them at the time of the "Get Ahead" Competition, when John had contacted us about becoming our London agent. John and Jean were Yorkshire people, originally from Sheffield, where John had worked in the spring-making industry. In middle-life, he and his wife had set up in business in Clerkenwell as importers and distributors of watch repair materials. We offered them a large discount for minimum purchases of at least one gross of every size of watch glass, for which he offered payment by return. The arrangement was acceptable to all of us, and we were to remain good friends for many years.

This was to be the only occasion on which John and his wife ever came to see us. The weather over that weekend was glorious, and on Sunday morning I took John to a popular beauty spot not far from our home. This was a viewpoint high above the Aire valley, from which stretched a wonderful panorama leading the eye towards the Yorkshire Dales. Miles of purple-capped heather moors led to distant mountain peaks beyond. We sat there silently for a while, admiring the breath-taking view. Then my companion spoke.

"Jack, how would you like to make clock mainsprings for me? I'll lend you the money to get started. You will not only have me as a customer but you'll also be able to sell through your existing watch glass outlets."

John was not only a main distributor of watch spares, but had for many years manufactured mainsprings for small clocks. I had seen his workshop, and his methods were rather basic. The work had become tedious and hard.

"I'm ten years older than you, Jack," he went on, "and need to take things easier," Then as an added incentive, he said.

"What's more, Jack, I'm prepared to supply you with my other watch spares at just over import price. That would increase the range of goods available to your customers. Then you wouldn't have all your eggs in one basket. I'll lend you the money to buy stocks - you can repay me over a couple of years. You can transfer all my stock of clock spring steel to your factory."

These two ventures - clock spring making and parts sales - meant borrowing the equivalent of what is, as I write, about £30,000.

'It's a lot of money to lend without security, John", I said. I am not sure whether it was because he knew that Agnes and I were Christians, but his answer was immediate.

"I trust you," he replied, "and you'll be doing me a favour."

After discussing the matter with our wives, we shook hands on the deal. The steel and stocks of spares arrived within the week. With help from my son David, who was on summer vacation from college, I quickly developed a semi-automated system of clock mainspring production. We produced a catalogue of our new products, which we sent to all our customers. We had diversified our business and almost overnight had created something that was to expand and be a source of income right into our semi-retirement. Our increased turnover had more than replaced our loss of watch-glass sales. Had all this been a fortunate coincidence, or had God really answered my prayer?

I was soon to know with certainty that God had taken me at my word.

14

Deliverance and healing miracles

Our larger watch-glass customers, all of whom dealt in general watch and clock spares, were interested in our clock mainsprings and placed orders with us. David soon proved adept at making them and soon built up a small stock of most sizes.

Friday was always our busiest day. We all worked frantically to complete the week's watch glass orders and get them into the post. My wife Agnes dealt with all personal callers, and had perfected an extremely effective formula for protecting me from unwelcome visitors.

On the first Friday on which we had the extra burden of clock spring orders, I was quite confident that I would remain undisturbed. I was soon proved wrong.

Suddenly, Agnes appeared at my side, looking quite excited. "There's someone from your past to see you - name of Robertson", she said. "He says you'll remember him better as 'Robbie.'"

"Never!" I gasped. "Show him in!"

Who could forget Robbie? Although twenty-five years had passed since our days together as Japanese Prisoners of War in Thailand I still remembered vividly the humorous repartee that had characterised him and made him the life and soul of the party. As he walked towards me - now twice as old as when we last met – I recognised his face instantly. Then came the shock. Gone completely was the mischievous sparkle that had accompanied the unceasing jollity and optimism I had known all those years ago. Instead, I was confronted with a staring, withdrawn look. It was a look that had been mine during the immediate post-war years. It spoke of fear, despair, and an awful darkness of mind and spirit. For a moment I relived that darkness, and a surge of pity went through me.

The pleasure of our reunion did not last long. Almost compulsively and with an apparent sense of urgency he poured out his story. Soon after demobilisation he had married and settled down, but then, for reasons he had failed to understand, depression had set in. This had eventually overwhelmed him completely. The arrival of his two children had brought light back into his life for a short time, but his depression had returned with renewed intensity. Increased responsibilities and financial burdens had made matters worse. He was now caught up in a vicious circle. Because of his inability to cope with life and with people, his income as a sales representative had diminished. His thoughts had become increasingly morbid, and I could see that suicide had begun to present itself as a way of escape.

He explained how he had located me. He had watched the "Get Ahead" T.V. competition in 1958, and now, some twelve years later, appeared to have stumbled upon me by accident. Although my heart went out to him, my mind seemed to go numb. He could see that I seemed to be fit and happy, and longed that I should help him. What should I say? How could I, in the middle of a busy morning, my staff constantly demanding my attention, explain the events which had brought me out of a darkness similar to his own? In any case, would just telling him make any difference?

I cannot remember what I did actually say to him. No doubt I used words intended to bring comfort and reassurance. Perhaps I offered friendship and hope. When he left half an hour later I felt sick inside. "Words!" I thought, "how useless and ineffectual in a situation like that."

As the following week progressed I forgot about Robbie's visit. As ever, there was no let-up in our watch-glass business. Our

106

customers continued to harass us as usual. They needed to keep their stocks up to date to avoid the expense of dealing piecemeal with orders for watch repair materials.

To my surprise, Robbie visited me again on the following Friday morning. He said that our talk of the previous week had been good for him. Could I not tell him more about what had happened to me? In the hour that followed I tried to unfold my story. I found it impossible to do this adequately or to bring real help to him in the sixty minutes we had available. As we shook hands and said goodbye for the second time, tears began to stream down his face. I remember seeing his look of abject despair. Anger welled up inside me as I thought: "The Japs are still beating him!" Suddenly, I found my right arm outstretched, my hand on his shoulder, and heard myself saying: "Go! I'll see you're all right!" Then Robbie turned on his heel and left.

"What on earth', I said to myself, "have I done! More to the point, what shall I do now?"

Indeed, what could I do? Almost immediately I thought of Bob, who had helped me in that amazing way all those years before. Then my mind turned to Brandon, through whom my life had been transformed by becoming a Christian. Thoughts of what to do occupied my mind throughout the weekend.

Back at work on Monday morning, I heard the enquiry bell ring at about ten o' clock. There was no time to answer it - the workshop door flew open and Robbie, uninvited, strode quickly across the room towards me.

"I've come to thank you!", he said, thrusting his hand into mine.

"For what?" I asked, completely confused.

"Can't you tell? Can't you feel it?" he almost shouted.

I could feel nothing. I had not experienced feelings like the ones Bob had brought to me since I had become a Christian. Yet it was quite clear that Robbie's depression had gone. He told me what had happened after he left on the previous Friday. Some fifteen minutes into his journey "something had begun to happen inside." He had felt compelled to find a church and tell God everything. He had not been inside a church for ten years. His whole being had then been filled with the power he had spoken of. The details of Robbie's encounter with God I shall never know, but he had been delivered instantaneously from his depression and despair. Often during the next few weeks Robbie could be seen in our parish church, browsing through the bookstall on his own. Shortly afterwards he obtained a new and more rewarding job. It was in the town of his origin in the North-East, near to family and friends. I have prayed that God would complete his work of healing, for I have not met Robbie since.

For me, many questions remained. Just how did Robbie receive his healing? If I, somehow, had been the agent, who then was the healer? Where did my old allegiance to Bob and my new-found faith in Christ fit into it all?

I stayed confused for months until, one day, God provided the answer.

I enjoy making things. The great thing about my business was that it had provided scope for my creative energy in thinking up new machines and processes. For twenty years I had been totally absorbed in developing and expanding my watch-glass business. Now that I had reached middle age and my family were grown up, I decided to seek more leisure time and look for ways to relax. My daughter Margaret had married in 1967. She and her husband Roger lived near Ferrybridge in south Yorkshire, where Roger was a power station engineer. My two boys were still at school. David, aged eighteen, was in the upper sixth form, Philip at age fifteen followed in his tracks at the same school

One thing I had never tried my hand at was carpentry. It was summer 1970, and when David and Philip had suggested that a dinghy would be a good thing to have on our summer holiday in West Wales, I decided to have a go at making one. I knew that Dick, my prisoner-of-war friend, was expert at building boats. He soon drew up a simple design for a flat-bottomed dinghy and cut out the panels for me. Philip and I collected them from Dick's home in Thirsk and I got down to work immediately. I had the boat finished by August, just in time for our holiday. We managed to secure it to the roof rack of our car, which only just coped with the weight of boat, roof rack, passengers and luggage. I recall that we had taken that caravan holiday just a couple of months before Robbie's visit.

Despite its flat bottom, the boat really did ride the sea well. My confidence in Dick to choose a good, yet simple design had been well-founded. Only a few miles from our caravan site we found a well-known spot where sands stretch out in a straight line for a great distance. On a good day the breakers would roll in endlessly. It was an ideal place for bathers and boaters alike.

My sons decided that riding the breakers, especially with dad in the boat, was the bee's knees! However, after the first day even that grew a bit tame - something more adventurous was called for. Anyone could ride the breakers nose first, they decided. The real challenge would be to ride them broadside on! At first we succeeded (great thrills!), but then, unexpectedly, a gigantic roller appeared. There was no time to turn into it - the boat lifted high into the air, turned over, and then crashed down on top of us. Bellowing with laughter, David and Philip emerged unscathed.

There was no such reaction from me. I had been sitting in the middle of the dinghy, and as it had turned over I had been thrown onto my back. As the boat followed me, one of the rowlocks crashed down onto my left knee. I writhed in agony from terrible pain in my joint. I remember walking up and down the beach for ages, rubbing and exercising my knee in an attempt to ease the pain. It was troublesome for the rest of the holiday, and was never really right after that.

The following February, some time after Robbie's visit, the real winter weather arrived. I awoke one morning to find snow all around. What I did not know was that, under the snow, my garden path was covered with ice. As I stepped out of the house my feet shot from under me. My leg twisted, and I fell heavily to the ground. Simultaneously I felt a sharp, searing pain in my left knee. I was unable to stand - the joint was partly dislocated. I enlisted the services of a well-qualified physiotherapist who put the joint back in place - a nightmare experience. He informed me that my cartilage was badly damaged. Over the next few days he visited me and massaged the knee, muscles and ligaments. Finally he had to admit that he was making no real progress, and held out little hope of future improvement.

His prognosis proved correct. As the weeks went by my muscles began to waste away and the knee joint started to get loose. After a few months the leg was thin and emaciated. Yet I did not approach my doctor to arrange for an operation for fear of the consequences to my business should I be absent for very long. I was the king-pin around which the business rotated. Only I knew the intricate machines and how to set them up. I had visions of everything falling apart. In retrospect, I doubt if my customers would have deserted me overnight. However, I continued to hope that the joint would strengthen. A Christian lady, a physiotherapist at a local hospital, showed me how to massage the limb. She also explained that I could strengthen my muscles by attaching heavy weights to my foot and then raising my leg up and down from a sitting position for several minutes each day. I did all this with no apparent result. One day my G.P., who was also a personal friend, met me in the street. It was early summer. I was leaning against a wall at the time, looking ridiculous, unable to move because my knee was locked. Shaking his head, he gave me a somewhat despairing look and said: "There's no blood supply to cartilage tissue, Jack. You'll have to have the operation."

I had become used to clicking my joint back into place on such occasions, much to the horror of my friends! However, after this I decided that I must try to arrange admission to hospital after Christmas, when most of my customers took an extended holiday.

One Saturday in early September I received a visit from Jane's brother - Bob's nephew. He was a keen supporter of Bob's work. Hearing of my knee problem he immediately pressed me to see Bob again. "He's getting on a bit now," he said, "but his gift is very powerful. I'm sure he will be able to help you."

At this point a remarkable thing happened. I became conscious of a quiet voice, very faint, speaking into my mind, which said: "Don't go. You're a Christian now. Go to the laying-on-of-hands service at your church next month."

Only once before in my life had I heard that voice. That had been after my terrible car accident over twelve years before. On that occasion, as now, I knew that the voice came from God.

The service of laying-on-of-hands had been fixed for mid-October. It was to be preceded by a talk on Christian Healing, to be given by a well-known speaker from London. Although I and one or two others from church were to be involved with the arrangements, the idea of receiving laying-on-of-hands for myself had not entered my head. So much for my faith! Yet now I was resolved to obey what I believed was an instruction from God. Meanwhile, I continued the daily massage and weightlifting.

The 'healing day' duly arrived. Two hundred people turned up to hear the speaker, and a further hundred arrived for the service. Among them was our daughter Margaret who had brought our six-months old grandson, Simon, for prayers. He was shortly to have a serious operation on his foot. As the time for ministry drew near, I felt I was much too tired to go forward, and my knee was aching badly. The absurd thought entered my mind that I was not in the right spiritual state for ministry after working hard all day. Margaret, however, much too embarrassed to go forward on her own, implored me to accompany her to the communion rail. As she knelt with her baby son for prayers, I remained standing. Yet it seemed that no-one would occupy my place! The thought flashed through my mind that I should kneel and receive a blessing. So I knelt down; hands were laid on me and a prayer was said. I wasted no time in returning home, glad to be able to take the weight off my knee.

That service of laying-on-of-hands had taken place on a Saturday afternoon. On the following Wednesday Agnes and I arrived home for lunch at our usual time of 1 p.m. I had barely entered the house when I felt a sudden tightening in my left knee, a distinctly unusual feeling which lasted only a fraction of a second. I called out to Agnes, who was already in the kitchen.

"Something's happened to my knee," I shouted.

"Pull the other one!" came the answer, in a note of disbelief.

Then I heard again that inner voice, quiet, but clear, as before. This time it said:

"You've put Christ in the right place. Reject all that is not of him."

My knee had been healed instantly. All my thigh muscles had been restored and my leg was completely strong again.

It has remained so ever since.

15

I make a mistake, and learn a lesson

"You've put Christ in the right place. Reject all that is not of him." After such a miraculous healing, how could I disobey those words? It did mean that I would have to renounce any allegiance to Bob, and refuse completely to take on board alternative therapies or medicines whose healing powers had their source in mysticism or Eastern religions. Over the years before becoming a Christian I had met many people who had claimed to have been healed by faith healers. Now I set my face against all such things. I made a promise to God from my heart that I would be obedient to his word to me. I began to realise the enormity of the spiritual battle that exists between the Church of Christ and the forces of evil. I began to sense also that I was being drawn into this supernatural spiritual battle. However, as yet I knew little of the countless ways in which Satan, the reality of whom the Church in general is loath to confess, seeks to frustrate God's plan for his creation.

Among the few people in our church who were interested in the healing ministry were Keith and Gladys. During the months following the miraculous healing of my knee, Agnes and I found ourselves with them quite a lot, and we soon became good friends. As chief accountant of a large company, Keith had a very stressful job. He would share his problems with me, and we would pray together about them. We also decided to attend the local swimming baths on a regular basis, which helped us to unwind and temporarily forget business matters. Gladys was extremely keen on the Christian healing ministry, and possessed real faith in Christ's power to heal through the Holy Spirit. She longed to be used in a "hands-on" way.

One day I received a telephone call from a friend at church. He was very concerned for his neighbour, a middle-aged lady who lived with her schoolteacher son. She was very depressed, and agoraphobic. Apparently she had not left the house for two years. My friend said he felt sure I would be able to help her. I decided that his reason for believing this was because I had stood alongside him some time before, when he had gone through a dark time himself. I was to realise later how the Holy Spirit, when he knows we are able to be used in a particular way, goes before us and prepares the ground so that he may act.

I asked Gladys if she would accompany me to see the lady. At this first meeting we explained the Christian basis for any claim to be of help. The lady was not a Christian, but was prepared to trust us and let us pray with her. As we prayed, we committed the whole matter to Christ, and arranged to call again the next evening. The deliverance (as I came to know it was) was simple and undramatic. On this second visit I found myself praying differently from before. This time I prayed with authority against the spirit of fear and depression that held her in their grip. I say "found myself praying", because at that time I did not really think of myself as having any ministry of deliverance. I prayed as came naturally to me, not realising that the Holy Spirit was using me in any special way.

The lady rang up early the next morning. "I'm all right," she said. "I'm completely healed. How much do I owe your church?"

Of course, I told her that she owed us nothing, and must get on with her life again. It was soon evident that the lady was indeed cured from her depression and agoraphobia. It was not long before she found employment with a local retailer. Because our paths did not cross, I never met her again.

Some five years later my wife came across her name in the obituary column of the local newspaper. There was to be an inquest.

Apparently she had taken her own life.

I recall quite clearly my feelings on hearing the news of that tragic death. Anger, frustration and guilt had overwhelmed me as I realised, some five years on, that we had never completed the work God had given us to do. The truth of Jesus' words recounted in Luke Ch.11, verses 24-26, when speaking about the man oppressed by an evil spirit, came home to me sharply. When the evil spirit had gone out of a man, said Jesus, it would travel over dry country looking for a place of rest, and finding none, would go back to its "house". Discovering it empty, clean and tidy, it would return, bringing seven other spirits worse than itself to live there. Then the person would be in a worse state than at the beginning. In helping that woman we had used the powerful name of Christ, and by his authority, in the power of the Holy Spirit, fear and depression had been driven out. Yet we had failed to bring to her the Christian Gospel. We had not counselled her or sought to discover the cause of her condition. We had not brought to her the complete healing that would have resulted from a life changed by becoming a Christian. It had not occurred to me that I had been in a situation just like hers after my depression had been dispelled by Bob. The difference had been that I, a regular churchgoer, curious to know by what means Bob had healed me, had been searching for Christ. Although that search had led to renewed darkness and even worse depression, I had finally been delivered. God had honoured his promise in the letter to the Hebrews, Ch. 11, verse 6, that if we believe that God exists and really seek to draw close to him, he will indeed reward us.

So what of demons and evil spirits? Do they really exist, even today? To Jesus they certainly were real; he took authority over them and cast them out "with a word". Very shortly after the events just related I found out for myself the reality of demons. It was as though I had been thrown in at the deep end into the deep, dark waters of occultism, that I might recognise, before embarking on any ministry to others, the extent of the sinister, hidden powers that Satan uses in his attempts to destroy us.

16

Another mistake, and I meet with demons!

Brandon, our vicar, spent much time and care each year in preparing candidates for confirmation. At the end of those many weeks of instruction he would invite two lay people to meet them. He would then disappear from the scene, having invited the candidates to ask questions they might consider difficult to ask him.

This story concerning the demonic had its beginning in such a meeting. Together with a very wise Christian lady I had agreed to try to answer any questions the twenty or so adult confirmation candidates might have prepared for us. Most had been straightforward, and related to the way in which being a Christian had improved the quality of our lives. Then, out of the blue, a rather striking lady - of indeterminate years, possibly forty-five to fifty years old - asked if she could put a question to us. She said that before starting the confirmation course she had undergone what she was sure was a real experience of God. Now it all seemed unreal. She inquired of us why that was.

We came up with all the usual "right" answers; faith does not depend on feelings, and anyway we all come to faith differently, and our experience is subjective, and so on. Then I made a statement - one of those "I found myself saying" ones. I told her that our faith can be clouded by any involvement with the occult, or belief in superstition etc., etc. After this she became quiet, and did not speak again. However, we were destined to renew our acquaintance later.

About this time, a young married couple, by name Jim and Kate, came to live just outside our parish. Previously, they had lived at the other side of Bradford and had attended a well-known charismatic church. They were well-known by those interested in charismatic renewal, especially by young people. Quite a few of our young friends had occasionally been invited to their home for fellowship. Many would come away full of the Spirit, speaking in tongues! It seemed that when Jim prayed with people, this quite often happened. One day Jim invited me to his house in order to meet a girl who had a compulsive behaviour problem, and whom he was trying to help. At the end of the evening Kate took the girl home, during which time two other friends arrived.

Kate returned in less than half an hour, and the five of us settled down to coffee and a chat. As our conversation developed, we found ourselves discussing the subject of tongues. At this point Jim turned to me.

"I can't understand, Jack," he said, "why you, so involved in the "healing" ministry, do not speak in tongues".

"To tell the truth", I replied, "I've never given the subject any thought".

As I pondered the matter I suddenly realised that in my mind were two strange words. They were a bit like Latin words. I told my friends about it.

"Oh!", said Jim, taking charge, "you need ministry! What we will do is stand in a circle and pray. At first we'll all pray in English, and then the four of us will pray in tongues, whilst you repeat your two words".

Jim's wife and their two friends had received the gift of tongues a long time before. We did exactly as Jim had told us. When the praying in tongues began, something started to happen to me. I had kept my eyes closed, and now I seemed to be looking down a deep well, at the bottom of which was a brilliant light. As I looked, the light began to coil upwards to the surface. Carried on the top of each coil was a word. I had been saying my two Latin-sounding words, but now new ones flooded spontaneously out of my mouth in a long stream! As they did so, my spirit became full of a joy such as I had never known before. This went on for a couple of minutes. I remember little of what happened next. I felt to be in a different world, and was praising God freely in my new tongue!

As I set off in the car for home I found myself singing in the Spirit! As I sang, I was aware that this was a different tongue from the one I had been using just previously. This was indeed "Latin-like", and gentle; the other had been stronger, and had an authoritative quality. I found later that this strong tongue came to me during times of deliverance ministry. Both tongues have remained with me ever since, although I do not place undue emphasis on these gifts. Nevertheless, I was to find out the value of tongues during the time of demonic oppression that was soon to follow. I believe that God gave me this gift in anticipation of the difficult experience that I would shortly have to face. I returned home wondering what I should tell Agnes. Actually, I allowed three years to pass before I shared with her the events of that evening. By then she had seen the Holy Spirit at work on many occasions.

One evening I received a phone call from the pastor of a parish a few miles away, who knew me fairly well. He asked if I would come over to discuss something too serious to speak about over the phone. When I met him the next day he explained that he had been approached for help by a lady who had appeared to be in awful mental anguish. At first he had thought that she had a deep anxiety problem. Then she spoke of symptoms that painted a different, more sinister picture. She said that after her fairly recent conversion to the Christian faith, frightening things had started to happen. Often, when she entered church, the cross on the communion table would appear to turn upside down. At other times, water seemed to run before her eyes. Sometimes a single day would seem like years, and she would hear voices in her head. There were other symptoms that I cannot recall. My friend had reluctantly come to the conclusion that the lady was occultly affected. Unfortunately he had no experience of dealing with such persons. For some reason my name had come to mind, and he had wondered if I would help him minister deliverance.

In retrospect, I know that I should never have agreed to his request. Up to that time, which was only a few years after being baptised in the Holy Spirit, I had never encountered people who were actively demonised. I was unaware that of three main areas in which Satan is at work against us, namely, rejection, sexual entrapment and occultism, of these the most sinister was the huge area of the occult, involving deliberate involvement with sorcery and Satanism. I was not to know what the causes of this woman's problems were, since I had no knowledge of her background or of her past because I had never had opportunity to discuss those things with her. At that time I did not know how vitally important it is to obtain a full confession from those seeking deliverance from any kind of bondage. Neither did I or my clergyman friend realise that the diocesan bishop had ruled that all cases of occult subjection be referred to him, in order that they might be dealt with by his chaplain specially appointed for exorcism.

So far in my experience people with whom I had been involved responded to prayer ministry, sometimes instantly and at other times after some weeks of counselling, always with another person alongside me. The idea of carrying out an exorcism had never occurred to me.

Another thing I was unaware of at that time was that those who have deliberately engaged in supernatural, occult practices, thereby entering willingly Satan's domain, put themselves out of the bounds of God's grace. It is when such people seek to become Christians that their torment begins. Satan is a deceiver and a liar. He works in darkness, seeking to keep his activities secret. In this area the average Christian may easily be fooled. The dimension in which spiritual warfare takes place may be outside the counsellor's experience and therefore be considered by him quite incredible.

My clergyman friend arranged a meeting at his house with the lady in question, to which I was invited. I soon discovered that my friend had no knowledge of how to go about deliverance prayers. Consequently, I had to give him brief directions before the lady arrived. Looking back, I realise how foolish and unwise we were to proceed further, being so much in ignorance of what deliverance ministry at this level could involve. I received a further shock when the woman arrived. Incredibly, she was the person who, during the confirmation classes at my own church some months before, had put to us the question about her loss of faith.

We moved into another room where we would remain undisturbed. My pastor friend, after saying a prayer for protection, addressed the demons in the woman. Immediately, her face contorted horribly, and she began to writhe and scream. My friend continued to command the demons to leave, and after some fifteen minutes she quietened down. We assumed that the battle was over. I was asked to say a prayer, and the lady left shortly afterwards. I remember the exhilaration that my friend and I felt at that time. How wonderful, we thought. to have claimed such a victory for Christ! Little did we realise that such had not been the case.

Next day I received a phone call from the pastor's wife. The lady we had prayed with had rung her, asking for further help. She had seemed to be in a very disturbed state. As the pastor was out of town, she had asked if I would see her. I agreed to meet her in church.

She explained that, although she had remained at peace for a few hours, her symptoms had then returned with renewed intensity. I spent half an hour trying to quieten her down. After saying prayers with her, I left for home. Some weeks later she contacted me again. Our pastor friend had decided not to be involved any further with her, and she implored me to help. I will not detail the events of the following weeks. Demons manifested endlessly through this woman, and would have continued to do so, had not help been received from a high-churchman priest who had a special ministry of exorcism. He was backed by a team of praying men and women of his own choice. It came to light that for very many years this woman had been involved in many types of magic and occult practices, and had engaged in illicit sexual relationships. Her deliverance was achieved through counselling, which eventually led to full confession, repentance and renunciation, followed by prayers of exorcism.

Following this, she agreed to receive Holy Communion regularly over a long period. Without confession, the earlier ministry had been useless. The door through which demons could enter had been left wide open. Due to her unconfessed sin, Satan had continued to claim his right to invade her soul. So I learned two things. Firstly, sometimes the dramatic response to confrontational exorcism as experienced in this case may be no more than the lifting up of the corner of a carpet under which may be hidden terrible evil. This may be so serious and deadly that it demands ministry from those whom God has really equipped for this work. The priest who dealt with this case was surprised that I had survived my encounter with the demons in this woman. I had been very conscious of God's protection during that time. An account and explanation of this would itself make a remarkable story. Secondly, I learned that the first approach to deliverance of occultly affected people must be through counselling under the Holy Spirit's leading, in order to reveal unconfessed sin and other hidden causes. Only when repentance, confession, renunciation and absolution have taken place can the work of closing the door permanently to Satan's activity be completed. This may be a long haul, one which may involve both mental and spiritual anguish. Satan does not relinquish easily his hold on those who once avowed allegiance to him.

Since that time I have had confirmation of the truth of what I have just said. I have spoken to several clergy who have been called to help people who have received "deliverance" ministry from those who think that all we need to do is to claim the power of the blood of Jesus and the authority of his name. Sadly, I have witnessed personally this type of ministry during large charismatic renewal meetings and conferences. Screams, audible throughout the hall, would be greeted by cheers from the onlookers. Knowing little of the things I have just warned about, they had assumed that the person had been dramatically and completely delivered. Unfortunately, the person's condition would often worsen later. I have prayed that such victims would eventually be fortunate enough to receive proper counselling and ministry, so that the causes of their condition might be fully exposed and dealt with.

Let me relate to you another happening which showed me the reality of demonisation. It occurred not long after the events I have just related. Again, it concerned someone who had deliberately involved herself with the occult, and who had then turned to the Church for help.

One day I received a telephone call from a clergyman in a neighbouring diocese. He asked me if I would accompany a young man on a visit to a psychiatric hospital at which a young woman member of his church was a patient. She happened to live in my parochial area.

Arriving at the hospital, we found this twenty-one year old girl in her room. She was in a suicidal state following her involvement with spiritism and ouija boards. She had tried to take her own life by slashing her wrists. Her first reaction was to embrace the young man, whom she knew, but then she retreated quickly.

"They're telling me to keep away from you," she said, "or else".

"Who's telling you?" we replied, "and or else what?"

"The voices. They'll do awful things to me and my family if you don't leave".

We managed to persuade her to trust us. Her wrists were bandaged where she had slashed them two days previously, and they were scarred from previous attempts. We inquired how her problems had started. She said that whilst playing at the ouija board a terrifying force had suddenly entered her. The table had been sent flying. Subsequently she had experienced nightmares, often several times in one night. One was of a wedding and a funeral proceeding together in church, where the cross on the communion table was upside down. Another was of a headless horseman chasing her in an attempt to kill her. Voices tried to persuade her to take her own life. They threatened dreadful retribution on the family if she refused.

Eventually we persuaded her to accompany us to the hospital chapel. Standing in the middle of the small room, we put our hands on her head and began to pray. She screamed violently. Then she tore the gold cross and chain from her neck and flung it across the room. She had struggled frantically with us. Our prayers had lasted only seconds.

When she came to her senses she had no recollection of what had happened. At this point I decided that the best thing to do was to contact a priest who, under the direction of the Bishop, was licensed to deal with such cases. The three of us agreed on this course of action. Then I said to my friend: "Let us give her to Jesus before we leave". After placing our hands on her shoulders, I asked him to pray. The girl collapsed almost immediately onto the floor, where she lay for some time, apparently lifeless. Then my friend asked her, calling on Jesus's name, to get to her feet. She did so, and straight away fell to her knees at the communion rail. There she confessed her sins to God in a loud voice, and asked his forgiveness. She asked my friend to read to her from the Bible, and this he did for some time. Then she returned to her room, and my friend and I went home.

The girl rang me from the hospital the same evening. She was hearing voices again, and her other symptoms were returning. I hurried over to see her, together with a lady from church. We were able to pray with her without any violent reaction. However, we insisted that she rang the priest whose telephone number I had given her earlier. She contacted him next day, and together they arranged to meet the consultant psychiatrist in charge of her case. He recommended that she underwent electro-convulsive therapy. This, he said, was usually successful in such cases. After all, did she really want to believe that she was possessed? She decided to have the treatment.

It was about a week later when, visiting another patient, I chanced to pass the girl's room. I looked in, and she welcomed me to her bedside. She was recovering from a dose of her shock treatment, and appeared to be quite without emotion.

"Do you still have the nightmares and hear the voices?" I asked.

"No!". she replied, "I don't! And those - she pointed to her Bible and pile of Christian books on her locker - are all rubbish!".

17

Temptations and curses – then God equips me

The time came when people would seek my help during business hours. A typical example was when Gladys arrived one morning accompanied by James, a twenty-one year old man who was in a suicidal state. His father had suffered terribly in Belsen during the Second World War. James was a near neighbour of Gladys, who knew his parents well. He had been in and out of hospital three times during the previous six months, and had been discharged again only that morning, but within the hour had sunk into deep depression. His treatment had been electro-convulsive therapy. He quickly sought out Gladys, who decided to waste no time before doing something about it. Having arrived at my enquiry office, they got no further than there. James protested strongly that there was no further point in living. I recall the anger I felt as I heard this. There and then we sat him on a stool and I took authority over the suicidal spirit that held him in its grip. We prayed further, and the Holy Spirit showed us other areas into which we needed to minister. James was delivered there and then. He remained free of depression and married a Christian girl some months later.

This sort of thing continued to happen regularly, but overall did not take up a great deal of my time. My business was in no way adversely affected. The fact was that those times of prayer and ministry were a blessing to me. Having said that, I became increasingly aware of a spiritual battle in my life, and of the fact that

Satan was looking for any opportunity to tempt me in order to bring me down. It was not long before he managed to do this to some small degree.

Our enemy will always attack those who are actively involved in the battle against him. Those who earnestly seek to bring deliverance and salvation to others must in no way presume that they are exempt from his attentions or immune from his power. As I had discovered during my encounter with the lady who had sought help from my clergyman friend and who had subsequently confessed to have been involved for years in occult practices, demonic spiritual power used against us through such people is real. Moreover, it is just as completely evil and destructive in its effect as the Holy Spirit of God is perfectly holy and upbuilding. God's nature is always to have mercy and to bring blessing. Satan's plan is to destroy us by any means possible. Through my encounter with that woman I received damage to my nervous system and to my spiritual health that continued to affect me over a long period. I received no help or ministry at either parish or diocesan level. It was by a strange route, too lengthy to describe, that I was eventually healed from its effects.

One of the weapons Satan uses against those involved in the deliverance and healing ministries is pride. We read in The Book of Proverbs, not that pride goes before a fall, as is commonly stated, but that "Pride goes before destruction, and a haughty spirit before a fall." (Proverbs 16, v.18) Equally effective weapons are found in the sexual realm. Through temptation, seduction and sensual desire, our natural weaknesses can be exploited. By the mid-1970s it was fairly common for people with spiritual problems to arrive unannounced on my doorstep. Also, in my position as churchwarden, many would seek my help with other matters. One day, a young housewife whom I had known since her teenage years, called for a chat. She had seen some of her friends receive a new experience of the Holy Spirit and his gifts. Would I, she asked, undertake a few one-to-one Bible studies with her, that she too might have that same renewal experience?

I agreed to give her the odd hour of my time on Monday evenings. Agnes was always around on these occasions. After a few weeks, during which time I had prayed with her, she did receive an anointing of the Holy Spirit. She became keen to accompany me on visits I was then making to women receiving treatment in psychiatric hospitals. I agreed to this, and enjoyed her company on these occasions. It was mid-summer, and she would arrive at my house dressed attractively in light summer frocks, her long black hair draping her shoulders. Looking back, I realise that I looked forward to these visits, and found her attentions flattering. Her sexual attraction, together with my own pride - for she was many years younger than myself - was leading me down a slippery slope. As time went by I realised that her parting embraces, hitherto just farewell hugs as practised by so many Christians, had become much more than that. I knew I was being trapped into a wrong relationship yet felt unable to do anything about it.

The following weekend, Agnes and I visited our friend John and Jean in London. On Saturday morning we delivered a consignment of clock mainsprings to their business in Clerkenwell, and spent the rest of the weekend with them at their bungalow in the suburbs. Following a rather heavy Sunday lunch, I decided to take a walk alone through the nearby park. The place was almost deserted, and very quiet. My mind soon turned to my awful situation. A frightening aspect of it was the sense of a dark force at work that was preventing me from taking any action. Then, in the quietness, the Holy Spirit gave me a command. There was no voice, just an instruction put into my mind. I knew that when I returned home I had to bring the wrong relationship to an end. How I was to do this I did not know. What I was absolutely sure about was that I had been given enough strength of will to overcome whatever held me in its grip. As I resolved to obey that conviction, I received a new infilling of God's love and peace.

My next appointment with my young friend had been fixed for seven o' clock on the following evening. At the time of her arrival 1 was seated at the piano, trying to relax and drive away my apprehension. As she entered the room I stopped playing, and looked her in the eyes.

"It's gone", she said and immediately went out of the room. She apologised to Agnes, and left. I told Agnes about all that had happened, and asked her forgiveness. Later she said that she had sensed something was wrong but had felt powerless to do anything about it. I know now that a seductive spirit had been at work. Such is the nature of such forces that they have a paralysing effect upon the mind. God must certainly have given Agnes to me for my wife. Her capacity to understand and forgive far exceeded that of the average woman.

I reflected on how the affair had ended. "It's gone!". What a strange thing to say! Quite plainly, an evil spirit had left. During the weeks during which the relationship had lasted, many people had come within my orbit whom I had been powerless to help because I had been outside the bounds of God's grace. It gradually became clear to me that this attempt to bring me down by seduction had been a definite plan of the enemy, and not merely the result of human weakness. The truth of this belief was to be revealed quickly, and very dramatically.

Very shortly after these events, in the middle of the night, the face of a young woman appeared to me, as in a dream. It was that of a girl whom I had met at a friends' house soon after my return from the Far East. I had known her when I was a teenager, when she was only a child. She had grown up to be an extremely attractive adult. A relationship had developed that lasted for a short while prior to my engagement to Agnes. It had been a very passionate affair. This was not highly surprising, since for five years I had had no contact with the opposite sex. Suddenly released from my P.O.W. situation, I was now emotionally and physically wide open to such an exciting relationship. It came to an end as Agnes and I felt ourselves drawn together at a much deeper level. What I was not to anticipate was that this girl would reappear in my life later, some two years into my marriage. Eventually, because of guilt feelings, I could not allow the relationship to continue any longer. Remember, I was not a Christian then, and this episode was part of the awful confusion and depression I experienced in those post-war years. Several years later, during a special time of ministry about which I will speak later, I was able to confess the whole matter to Agnes.

Back to the dream. The face of this lovely girl, as she had been all those years before, appeared for what seemed only a second before it changed to that of Satan himself! A horrible black mass, the details of which I cannot recall, spat out the words, 'I'll kill you!'. At that point all the life started to drain from my body. I found myself crying out with the weakest of voices, "Jesus, Jesus!", whereupon the face vanished, and I awoke.

Next day I seemed to be perfectly well. What I did not realise then was that Satan had put a curse on me. He had used his perfect right to do so, namely, unconfessed sin.

Unaware of the curse, I continued to live life as before.

Not many weeks elapsed before sinister things began to happen. One evening, my younger son was working on his old car. It was dark, and Philip was working late to complete the welding work he had begun earlier. He was working on an open space at the side of the garage, a built-up area standing three feet above the garden. On my return home from an appointment that evening I walked down the drive to see how he was progressing. As I did so, he re-lit his welding torch ready to continue with the job. I quickly shielded my eyes from the damaging rays. Moving quickly in order to get behind him, I found myself striding into mid-air, dropping sideways headfirst into the garden. Three feet below was a rockery, and as I twisted in an attempt to regain my balance, I landed on my right shoulder among the boulders. Had I landed on my head instead of my shoulder, I might well have been killed. I was in agony next day, and over the years the pain in this shoulder got progressively worse. More about that later.

A few weeks after that incident I awoke with a severe pain in my right abdomen. It felt like a knife digging into me just under the skin. By the end of the week, spots had begun to appear on my lower body, and a visit to my doctor revealed that I had shingles. The symptoms rapidly grew more severe, until an area some six inches wide all round my body was affected. My G.P. said it was the worst case he had ever seen. I became terribly ill and was confined to bed for many weeks. I was in great pain and discomfort and could not lie down properly because of the suppurating red mass that covered my body. During that period I had to drag myself to my factory on several occasions to attend to production problems. The memory of that time is now just a blur.

Eventually I recovered from my illness and, remarkably, have suffered not the slightest sign of the disease ever since. However, other nasty things were soon to happen. A particularly unpleasant one occurred at the time of my elder son David's wedding. In order to get to the wedding reception, I needed to extricate my car from a tricky position in the church car park. This involved reversing the car with the steering wheel on full lock. As I did so, the whole of the nearside suspension collapsed. The strut, or stay, that had held it in position had sheared at the end. I obtained a new part without difficulty, and returned two days later to carry out the repair. As I removed and inspected the offending strut, a chill ran through me. For at the point of breakage there was only about a quarter of an inch of bright metal to be seen. The rest had sheared long ago, and was covered with rust. The implication was frightening. It was plain that, during the two and a half hours' motorway journey to the wedding, the failure of that tiny piece of metal could have spelt death for myself and my four passengers. It had been the manoeuvre of reversing, with the front wheels turned almost at right angles that had caused the final break.

It was a lovely summer evening, and I had almost completed the job in an hour. All that remained for me to do was screw the hexagon nut onto the bolt that secured the strut to the car body. I had run the front wheel onto a stepped ramp to give me plenty of room to work. The job was soon finished. Now I had to get the car off the ramp and onto the ground.

As well as the ramp I had used a jack for extra safety. The obvious thing to do now was to jack the car up higher and remove the ramp, and then lower and remove the jack itself. Instead of doing this, I decided, unaccountably, to remove the jack first and then run the car off the ramp, step by step. I unscrewed the jack until it was just clear of the chassis, and then put out my hand to remove it. Usually I would have done this by grasping the base and pulling it clear. Inexplicably, I got hold of the top. At that precise moment the car moved down the ramp one step, trapping the first finger of my left hand between the jack and the chassis. One and a half tons of car pinned it down.

When eventually my hand was released, I saw that my finger was in an awful mess up to the first joint. After waiting hours in casualty at the local hospital, I managed to persuade the surgeon not to amputate the end of my finger. He removed shattered pieces of bone and the nail bed. I left the hospital in great pain, my hand swathed in massive bandages. It was eight weeks before it was completely healed.

The catalogue of disasters continued. On a physical level these were bad enough (they included the development of an enormous boil in my nose which responded only slowly to anti-biotics), but then a sense of spiritual oppression seemed to overtake me also. Things came to a head on one Sunday morning when I had agreed to undertake an exorcism of a clergyman's wife during a Holy Communion service. A few hours prior to the ministry time I had spoken to the lady concerned. She had been told by an ordained person that I as a layman would not be able to help her. I had come away from that meeting feeling completely condemned and inadequate. Knowing what I do now, I would at that point have cancelled any attempt to proceed with the deliverance of that person. In the event, I was unable to exercise any spiritual authority, for condemnation had overwhelmed both myself and the person I had agreed to help. I sank into terrible depression, and found myself crying out to God.

Little did I expect help to arrive as quickly as it did! About noon next day, an acquaintance of mine who worked in a business next to my own called to see me. He was a rather extrovert Christian. I met him only infrequently on occasions when he brought me watch-glass work.

"Still on top of the world, Jack?" he asked breezily.

"Not today, I'm afraid, Garry", I replied, and then briefly explained why.

"We can't have that, Jack," he said, and left.

The very next day I received a telephone call from the pastor of Garry's non-denominational church, a man I'd heard about but never met. I knew that he and his wife had exercised a powerful counselling and deliverance ministry for many years. People had been led to them from all over the country, and even from abroad. Bill (not his real name) and his wife had always made a point of never seeking people out, and their telephone number was ex-directory. Nearly always, it seemed, they had found themselves helping church leaders or clergy.

"I believe God wants me to help you," he said. "Are you prepared to come along?". I was only too pleased to accept.

My first meeting with Bill was quite different from what I had expected. He was a quiet, unassuming man in his fifties, and he greeted me warmly in a northern accent. His counselling room was in his own home, and was very sparsely furnished. I waited, expecting to receive a session of high-powered ministry. Instead, he asked me to outline briefly the story of my life.

The two hours Bill had set aside for me soon passed. He interrupted me only occasionally. At the end he said: "Well, Jack, you certainly have met Satan in a big way. I feel sure God wants to use you in the same ministry as myself."

We arranged another appointment ten days ahead. This time, I thought, I'm bound to receive the ministry! Looking back at that day, I realise that a new peace had already come over me. However, the ministry was still not forthcoming. Instead, Bill gave me a testimony of his own, relating to an experience shortly after he was ordained. Great things had begun to happen to him. He had been baptised in the Holy Spirit, and many of the spiritual gifts had manifested through him. There were, however, things in his life of which he was ashamed, and which were keeping him in complete bondage. So much so, he told me, that when he ascended the pulpit stair to preach to his congregation, he felt convicted in his heart that he was unfit to do so. This had led him into severe depression from which he could see no way of escape. He had even considered giving up the ordained ministry.

Eventually the church elders decided that Bill should take time off and rest. They arranged for him to attend a clergy conference in Wales. Bill told me that for the first three days of the conference nothing penetrated his brain. Darkness still covered him like a cloud. On the fourth day, suddenly, he heard words that not only reached his brain, but which reached deeply into his heart with the certainty of truth. They filled him with such joy as only words borne by the Spirit can! The words were from Ezekiel Ch.36, v.25: "I will sprinkle clean water upon you, and you shall be clean from all your uncleanness, and from all your idols I will cleanse you. A new heart I will give you and a new spirit I will put within you; and I will take out of your flesh the heart of stone and give you a heart of flesh. And I will put my Spirit within you, and cause you to walk in my statutes and to be careful to observe my ordinances."

Bill knew that this promise of a pure heart was for him. As he accepted it he was delivered from the cause of his depression and began a life of anointed service for God. He was to bring similar deliverance to countless others over many years. Bill was convinced that a pre-requisite for my life was that I too should know the reality of those scriptures, and be rid of spiritual encumbrances within myself that would prevent my having an authoritative ministry under God. He told me to return home and search the scriptures to find out what they had to say to me about having a pure heart. We arranged appointments at fortnightly intervals over six weeks.

What happened next I found quite amazing. It was as if I were being led around the Bible by an unseen hand. I found myself reading scriptures in both New and Old Testaments, passages that hitherto had been unknown to me, but which had a strange ring of truth. On my visits to Bill I found that I was able to expound these verses with an insight and authority that amazed us both. Almost two months went by, and still I continued to receive proof in my heart that God is able to cleanse and strengthen us through our faith in Christ. Agnes had become aware of changes in me and of the Holy Spirit at work within her also. This enabled her to share inner hurts which we were able to bring before God together.

Three months had passed, and I still had no idea of what the end of all this would be. After all, I had only wanted to be free from condemnation and depression, and up to now I had received no real ministry. Yet I had to admit that I felt a great peace and that my depression was virtually gone. I decided to pray earnestly that I might receive the "pure heart" that Bill longed I should have.

Very shortly afterwards, my eyes lighted on some verses in The Book of Jeremiah. They were verses I had never heard before, though now I find that they are very well-known. They are in Chapter 29, verses 11, 12 and 13. As I read them, God appeared to be speaking directly to me, saying: "I know the plans I have for you, says the Lord, plans for welfare and not for evil, to give you a future and a hope. Then you will call upon me and come and pray to me, and I will hear you. You will seek me and find me; when you seek me with all your heart."

I was convinced now that God could do for me what he had done for Bill all those years before. So at my next meeting with him I told him of this, and asked him to minister to me accordingly.

"It's not like that, Jack," he said. "It's really all up to you. So get on your knees, here and now! Imagine you are at the foot of the Cross, where Christ died for you. Remember that he is alive and equal with God in spiritual authority and power. Therefore tell him that you want a heart that is emptied of all self-seeking and of everything that displeases God. Give him your fears, condemnation and all the other hurts for which other people are responsible. Invite Jesus into your heart with the longing that a bride has for her bridegroom. The Bible tells that the Church is the Bride of Christ."

So I did exactly that. I cannot remember my words, but the experience is still vivid to me. I had barely finished speaking when Bill said:

"Who put a curse on you, Jack?"

I racked my brain without success in an attempt to remember any incident when that had happened to me. I failed to recall that awful nightmare experience when Satan told me he would kill me. I had not then recognised it as a curse. I did recall it some years afterwards, as I will recount later.

Without wasting any more time, Bill broke the power of the curse. He had recognised its power over me through a word of knowledge that God had just given him. I felt peace flood through my soul. Bill went on to explain that I would feel progressively stronger spiritually as the months went by, because now Christ was really able to dwell in my heart by faith. As the months passed I was indeed aware of a transformation taking place, of becoming a stronger, more confident person. I was even more certain of Christ's power over the forces of evil.

It was around this time that I retired from the position of churchwarden, a post I had held for nine years within my local church. The Vicar thought it a good idea that I should consider the idea of becoming a Lay Reader. Accordingly I attended a diocesan course stretching over six weeks. The course over, I was asked to write a short account of why I wanted to enter the lay ministry. A week later I was interviewed by a panel of three people, a clergyman and two lay persons. From the onset of my twenty minute interview the questions put to me had no bearing on any ministry as a Lay Reader. "Tell us," the clergyman asked, "what you know about exorcism." I immediately gave the "correct" answer. "All cases of occult subjection must be referred to the Bishop!", I said.

"Yes, yes, Jack," he replied, impatiently, "but what we really want to know is your own experience of that sort of ministry. You really are not interested in preaching sermons, are you? We know that you could give a good Christian testimony if asked to do so. But come on, do tell us what you know about exorcism!"

I discovered later that these three people had known nothing about. me prior to the interview. They would have seen my short written account, and spoken about me with the clergyman who had led the diocesan course I had just completed. However, thinking that they must have gained some information about me, I recounted some of the happenings recorded earlier in this book. When I left the room I received what was almost an embrace from the diocesan course leader. Then he said:

"God says: 'People will come to you on a conveyor belt'."

The implications of this did not sink in. Later, however, this statement turned out to be prophetic, and was recognised as such by the clergyman who had said it. Returning to my parish, I awaited the report that was to follow and which my vicar eventually read to me. It intimated that I should be "trained" in the ministry of healing. There was no mention of my becoming a Lay Reader, and equally no mention of exorcism or deliverance. It was much later that I recognised the reason for this. That a lay person should be allowed to exercise a ministry of deliverance within the Anglican Church was, in my diocese at least, quite out of the question at that time. So the word "healing" had been used in the report, and the truth compromised. Sadly, this sort of compromise is, in my experience, found throughout the Established Church. Not only does the Church fail to preach a powerful, full Gospel, in which recognition of the spiritual battle against Satan is acknowledged, but it engages in compromise and secrecy. Most Bishops appoint a chaplain for deliverance within the diocese who, in my experience, is usually of high-church persuasion. They generally insist that all known cases of occult subjection be referred to them. However, this information is not generally known.

Some time later, at a weekend conference on the subject of Christian healing, it was stated openly by a Church dignitary that, following my attendance at a diocesan course, it had been discovered that I had a ministry of deliverance. The effect of receiving this news in such a manner staggered me. When I protested my ignorance of ever realising that I had such a ministry, my statement was received with scorn. Yet, I had truly believed that what I had been doing during the previous years was only part of Christ's healing work in the Church. I had just longed to bring people out of darkness into light, so that what had happened to me might happen to them also.

Thereafter, I had two long talks with the Archdeacon. He pointed out that what I really needed was encouragement, not training. Unfortunately, this help was not forthcoming. I received no support at diocesan level, for this would have meant that the Bishop would have to be informed and his permission given - and there was no hope of this. At the time I naively imagined that I had the establishment's blessing to minister to people if and when God led them to me. There was no support at parish level, because this was not a ministry in which my vicar had ever been involved. Although on more than one occasion I asked for help and support, this never arrived.

Nevertheless, things began to happen fairly quickly. One after the other, people began to arrive on my doorstep as if on a conveyor belt, as predicted.

18

God's protection and power revealed

All those who asked to see me appeared to have had a similar experience - an inner conviction that I would be able to help them. They arrived by unexpected routes. Often I would receive a phone call from someone urgently seeking help. Or I might find myself alongside someone in crisis - apparently by chance - that led to my being able to help them. These happenings occurred with such frequency that it had to be more than mere coincidence. I soon became aware that the Holy Spirit was directing people to me. In no way did I need to seek out people to help. Furthermore, I became increasingly conscious of the Holy Spirit's presence. Only now do I realise that I did not take these happenings seriously enough, or consider that God might want me to work full-time in Christian ministry.

One weekend, a remarkable happening took place that should have shaken me out of this complacency. It happened during a conference on Christian Healing, at the end of a Holy Communion service. With two other lay people, I had been asked to take part in the Laying-on-of Hands ministry which was to follow. The clergyman who had presided over the communion service first laid hands on each of us in turn. He turned to me last, and as he did so, he suddenly said, in a voice audible to the hundred or so people present, "Thank you, Lord, for saving Jack from death by Satan, and for this vision of your angels surrounding him, with their spears facing outwards."

One would expect that such a supernatural pronouncement, made through that quiet man, who was a dignitary of the Anglican Church, would have filled me with awe and fear. In fact, it had no such effect on me. It did, however, reassure me of God's protection, something that has remained with me ever since, even through the darkest times. I was still pressing on with improving my business by developing more sophisticated production techniques. From that time on, my days became more and more crowded. Many were the occasions when, at work, I would "down tools" to minister to people with problems ranging from suicidal thoughts, depression, to demonic symptoms. All this was unknown to my church at either parish or diocesan level. As a consequence, I had little or no help. There must be countless churches within the Anglican Communion where just a few individuals are fighting alone to release people from evil forces. This is because the Full Gospel of Christ is rarely preached - the spiritual battle being theoretical and doctrinal rather than something that is actually experienced. Consequently, in these churches the power and authority of God is not present. The tragedy is that there is so much deliverance work to do, with so few people equipped to do it.

The deliverance ministry carries a hidden danger in that even the most committed of us can grow to "enjoy", in the natural sense, our spiritual ministry. We must beware any sense of pride that would spring out of seeing people brought out of darkness. Deliverance is the Holy Spirit's work, and the glory must go to Christ. After deliverance has taken place, further identification and elimination of underlying causes can present an equally huge problem. This work is less dramatic, yet needs a range of counselling skills to be exercised by people who possess real Christian love. In my own experience I know of people who have monopolised the lives of many carers for months and even years. This has exposed a problem that would justify the setting up of full-time ministries, with their consequent demands on accommodation and financial support.

A time came when I was called upon to help certain clergy outside my own parish. I found this a somewhat awesome experience, as some of the men concerned were not parish priests, but dignitaries of the Church. These were true men of God who had found themselves in circumstances that had robbed them of confidence due to oppression, or condemnation by others. The forces at work were sinister and had brought these good men to a place of torment, which had affected their physical health also.

A common factor in these cases was that I was called upon at a moment's notice. There was no counselling involved, and on most occasions not much listening. I was just asked to pray! In one case where I actually was asked to listen to details of a relationship problem, the more I listened, the less I felt able to cope. The Holy Spirit fell on these people on each occasion as soon as I started to speak, and they were delivered. In some cases there was much weeping involved, and much praise for God as they gained their release through the power and authority of Christ. I talked with one of these clergymen later, and analysed the insidious way in which he had found himself trapped in an evil situation from which he had been unable to escape. He remarked that those who had experienced the reality of Satan's ability to lead us into torment and bondage could have no doubt of the truth of the Gospel.

I began to see that, up to this point in my life, wherever deliverance had occurred it had verged on the miraculous. There had been no prolonged counselling on my part, rather, the Holy Spirit appeared to have been at work beforehand, and had done all the work virtually independently of me. I had merely been an agent who had told Satan, within the authority of Christ, to loose his hold on the person. I had then asked God's Spirit to minister to the one who had been released. Sometimes I had been given special words to say. Once I asked that God would put a wall of protection round a certain clergyman who felt condemned and unable to preach in the presence of his superiors. Within days he had visited me at work to tell me that the wall indeed was there, and that the condemnation was gone.

I have often wished that all my cases of deliverance could have occurred in that same way. However, the Spirit blows where he wills. It is difficult for God to work in churches that would quench the Spirit's power through unbelief, or deny that he has any ministry within the whole body of Christ. That, together with tradition, human weakness, jealousy and fear amongst clergy assure the continuance of a divided, passive and ineffective Church. Yet sometimes the Spirit can work despite us. Not long after my involvement with the afore-mentioned clergy I found myself in a church where, at the end of a Good Friday meditative service, a lady was found slumped in her pew. At first it seemed that she had fainted, but it was soon seen not to be the case. I recognised that she was paralysed with fear. A nurse, a highly spiritual woman, prayed with her, with no result. Then she said to the clergyman standing nearby, "I believe she is under Satan's power." "Then pray again," the clergyman instructed. She proceeded to ask God to deliver her. The lady remained in an apparent trance. At that point, speaking directly to Satan, I took authority over his demonic power of fear at work in the person, and loosed her from Satan's grip. I found myself taking her by the hand and leading her out of the church. She began to speak of strange things such as I had heard from those who had been involved with the occult. I took her home, and on Easter Sunday she asked me to visit her. When I did so, I felt I had to direct her to Paul's letter to the Romans, Ch. 6. This speaks about dying with Christ, that we may be risen with him in righteousness of life. I said a prayer with her, and left. On Tuesday morning she rang me, and said, "I have confessed to God that I am a - and a - (she named two sins), and now I am telling you as well. A dark cloud has lifted, and the depression I've had for over two years has gone".

Later she told me that, as she lay on the pew, she had known that only I could help her. I do not recount that statement out of any sense of pride, because in no way did I wish then, nor do I wish now, to appear superior to any other Christian. The clergyman who had been present thought I had "taken over" the situation. I can understand that it must have been very embarrassing for him. Yet why are we, clergy included, often unable to practise what we preach? Why are we often unable to rejoice when we see God using others to heal, deliver or whatever? Do we not want all the glory to go to him? I realise now that what I possess is a ministry gift, not a spiritual gift such as healing, discernment of spirits, prophecy etc. My utter certainty of spiritual authority over evil has been realised, as you will have seen, out of much suffering for Christ over many years.

In the late 1970s business had become a chore. It was becoming harder to make a living because of foreign competition. Now, at sixty years old, I wished I could retire. Had I known what lay ahead in a couple of years time, I would indeed have tried to sell my business, together with the lease of the premises, which still had some nine years to run. I would have been able to pay off my overdraft at the bank - at that time £7,000 - and concentrate on my Christian work. Most of the money that my wife and I had ever earned we had spent on machinery and stock. Over a period of twenty years we had put £50,000 into the business. In 1980 we were to see the quite sudden advent of the electronic watch, with its battery-driven quartz movement and flat real glass. From that time onwards we were to witness the disappearance of the convex, acrylic watch glass that had been at the heart of our business. Our production machinery would be unwanted, and the money invested over all those years would be lost.

19

God, in Christ, heals young and old alike!

How easy it is, with hindsight, and after disaster has struck, to recognise clearly the human weaknesses, temptations and wrong decisions that have brought about our undoing. Only when it is too late do we long to be given a second chance!

The maxim which says that to be forewarned is to be forearmed is nowhere more applicable than in our battle against Satan. Do you remember Bill? He was the clergyman who had been used to free me from self-condemnation and who had led me to understand how to receive a pure heart. This had not meant that I had to become "holier-than-thou". My mind and spirit had needed to be healed of hurts received from others, as well as from things within me that were not of God - impurity, pride, greed, bitterness, jealousy etc. Yet this great acquisition was in large degree to be lost! In conversation later, Bill spoke of the many ways in which our enemy sets traps for us. Of all the things he said to me, what I am going to relate to you now I found hardest to believe. Yet, only a short time later, I was to go through an experience that would confirm absolutely the truth of what he had told me.

Bill had been involved in deliverance in all its forms for over twenty years. His understanding of the enemy's wiles had been achieved at considerable cost in terms of physical stress and spiritual discipline. I had come to accept what he said with absolute seriousness. Many Christians are familiar with the passage in Ephesians Chapter 6 about spiritual warfare, and believe quite seriously that Satan does roam around like a roaring lion, seeking whom he may devour. Yet the dangers of involvement in this warfare only become real when actually experienced. In the supernatural realm - the "heavenly places" where the war is - there are two opposing hierarchies. One has God at its head, the other is under the rule of Satan. The battle against spiritual death has been won for mankind through Christ's atonement on the Cross. Nevertheless Satan will continue to pursue until the end of time his objective of preventing as many people as possible from recognising the truth of the Good News. He will oppose all who are on the side of God. God has legions of angels deployed to protect us, and this is real and Biblical. So is the reality of Satan's demonic forces intent on destroying us. Bill stressed that the more effective we become in our ministry, the more attention we will merit from our enemy. Then he will set out to trap us, and this will apply especially to those with new ministries. He will plan ahead, preparing to put his plan into action. God will do the same, and prepare for us a way of escape. Unfortunately, because we often have no support from other Christians, and because we have not stayed close enough to God in our daily walk, we lack the strength of will to choose that escape route even when we recognise it. When we have been weakened spiritually, mentally and physically, Satan brings in all his demons in order to finish us off. When Bill told me this I found it difficult to believe. Yet I was soon to find myself in such a position, and I thank God that Bill was there to help me out of it. Let me relate my story.

The year 1980 was a good one for our business. Our sales increased considerably, and we soon discovered that one of our two large foreign competitors had gone bankrupt. I wrongly assumed at the time that this was because they had cut prices too much so that their business had eventually gone to the wall. I was to discover later that the real reason was the advent of the digital watch and the beginning of a new era in the watch industry. This was to revolutionise the watch-glass business. The change had first begun in the U.S.A, followed by Europe. As usual, the U.K. had lagged behind. If only I had been aware at the time of the change taking place, I would have done something about it. As it was, I continued

144

to produce the standard types of acrylic plastic watch glasses that had been our mainstay for years. Then, almost overnight, the convex watch glass went out of fashion. In its place came the completely flat type, made from real glass, except in the case of very cheap watches. As a consequence, our sales fell by a third by mid-1981, at which point we were rapidly losing money. In order to avoid insolvency we would need to sell the lease on our factory and make some of our staff redundant. The prospect of moving all our machinery and reinstalling it in new premises presented a colossal task. Because I had designed and made most of our machines myself, only I know how to dismantle and reassemble them.

In my spiritual life, too, things began to go dreadfully wrong. For many years I had ministered to many people within the Church. Most were lay people. Some, however, were ordained clergy who occupied fairly important positions in the Anglican Church. I knew much about the private lives of all these people. This was knowledge I had come by in my role of bringing God's light into dark situations. Over the years I had made it a rule to record nothing, but there were things in my heart that I had kept hidden. Quite suddenly, confidential matters surfaced from an unexpected quarter. For obvious reasons I cannot relate anything of what followed. Suffice it to say that because I was aware of certain happenings, some of which had involved opposing factions in the Church, I was subjected to pressures to tell what I knew. All this happened at a time when my business worries were overwhelming me, and I was physically and mentally tired. To make matters very much worse I found myself involved in helping a lady who had a severe spiritual problem. It was a situation in which I should have received help. Instead of this, I pursued the matter alone, and found myself in a trap I had never anticipated. Although I was presented with a means of escape from this situation, I found I did not have the will to take it. I soon became aware of forces at work around me that were bent on destroying the Church from within. I became subject to forces of temptation, accusation, condemnation and many other evil pressures that temporarily destroyed any ministry I had for Christ. Then, just as I could see no end in sight and no escape from temptation, help came from someone who had discerned the nature of my problem. He was the clergyman who had been given that remarkable vision of God's angels protecting me. He ministered to both myself and Agnes. As a result, the reality of my relationship with God was partially restored. The worry of our business situation was still with us, however, and I still retained a legacy of condemnation because of the "unwisdom" of my actions in that evil situation within the Church. Yes, God can bring us into the light, he can equip us, cleanse our hearts so that he can use us. Yet we can "blow it" and negate any ministry he would exercise through us. In my case it had been spiritual pride that had brought me down. Of course, I did not recognise this until long afterwards.

Yet, over the next few years, God was to build me up again and lead me into a deeper, more effective form of deliverance ministry. Sadly this did not happen until I had gone through much more suffering. For the moment, however, I had come out of that period of darkness and regained my absolute assurance of Christ's authority. I have close friends who smile when I tell them - apparently very regularly - of my "utter certainty" of this fact! Then, as if to assure me of his forgiveness for mishandling things, God soon chose to use me as a channel of the very authority of which I spoke with such apparent conviction! He did so by performing what I see as nothing less than a miracle.

One Sunday, a lady (whom I shall call Freda) approached me after morning service. She told me that a dear friend was seeking help for her daughter whose three-year-old boy, Mark, was dying of leukaemia. Freda had said that I was the only person she really knew well who believed that prayer could bring healing. I told her immediately that my gifts did not lie in that direction. Had the problem been depression, I said, I would have been only too glad to help. I felt that this case was just not for me.

Now Freda was not the persistent type, so it was quite out of character when, a week later, she approached me again with the same request. Once more I gave the same answer. However, during the following week a strong thought came into my head. I felt that I should tell this young mother about Jesus, and tell her that if she became a Christian, she would be able to cope, even if her boy were to die. For Mark had been given only a short time to live. So Freda arranged a visit for the following week. She and I met on the Thursday afternoon, and had a short prayer time in the car before approaching the house. That first meeting with Mark's mother is vivid in my memory. When she opened the door to her bungalow she had Mark in her arms. He was a pathetic small bundle, pale almost to the point of whiteness, and completely without hair as the result of chemotherapy.

Freda and I sat down on a settee opposite the two of them, and I proceeded to explain the Good News of Christ, and how, if she became a Christian, the Holy Spirit would come to her. I told her that God's love would bring peace in place of her present despair; that even if Mark died, she would be able to cope and know the uplifting presence of Christ. In silence, she listened to every word. Then, quietly, she said: "I still want you to pray."

I realised later that by saying those words she had put Jesus on the spot. It was as if she had said: "I've heard what you've said about this Jesus - all right then, tell him to do something!"

I walked over to where they sat, and asked Freda to join me in laying hands on the heads of both mother and child. As we did so, I was filled with an inner knowledge that the child was in Satan's grip. Full of anger against him, I took authority over this evil and rebuked the illness in the name of Jesus Christ. I cannot - as is usual - recall the exact words I used. Yet as I did so, both Freda and myself felt the life draining from our bodies! This apparently showed upon our faces. Without further conversation we said goodbye and left.

For a while Freda and I sat in the car in silence. We were both bathed in perspiration! As we moved off, we decided that, somehow, God had heard our prayers and that Mark and his mother had received a blessing. How weak our faith really is! We had not believed that what we had asked for would actually happen!

The following weekend was Bank Holiday, and Agnes and I took a week's break in the Yorkshire Dales. On the first day of our return to business the 'phone rang at about 10.00 a.m. It was Mark's mother.

"I took Mark to hospital in Leeds last Thursday," she said, "for the usual tests. Amazingly, the consultant told me that he could find nothing wrong with his 'blood'. She sounded overjoyed. Very soon afterwards she became a Christian, and Mark began later to attend our Sunday Schools. He now has a university degree, and is quite fit. His mother became a valuable member of her church's healing ministry group. As I look back over the events that had accompanied Mark's healing I realise that the Holy Spirit must have gone before us, preparing and clearing the way so that he himself could work. Both Freda and I had been led to act in a way that had been quite untypical of both of us. The mystery is that God is able to use us and glorify his name through us. This remarkable and joyful happening was a confirmation of the Biblical promise that signs and wonders will follow the preaching of the Gospel.

As that year progressed, our business rapidly declined. I eventually sold my lease and moved into a small industrial unit five miles out of town. The move, together with the installation of my machines etc. was, despite help from my sons and others, an extremely exhausting experience. Sadly, we had to lose a third of our staff. Agnes, despite her worsening heart condition continued to work alongside me.

Then one morning, whilst sitting at my work-bench, I felt an awful sickness come over me. Never had I experienced such a feeling in my life before. It was a sick-tiredness I just cannot describe. I was unable to sleep properly - anyway, I just had to keep on working. Then the time arrived when I was no longer able to work. Terrible pains had begun to invade my body; redhot, searing pains in all my joints and muscles. Eventually I was forced to retire to bed. By this time my head thumped and ached, and I was still unable to sleep. A consultant orthopoedic surgeon was called in, but he was unable to diagnose my condition. I underwent multiple X-Rays and blood tests, and spent ninety minutes under a body-scanner at the nearest city hospital, but in each case nothing was found. Confined to bed, my condition deteriorated even further. As well as my intense pain, numbness now began to set in, and I found myself unable to close my hands. Every few days I had to be taken by car to my business in order to set up the machines. Eventually every nerve in my body appeared to be affected. I was unable to fasten my shirt collar or feel anything at all with my fingers. I felt hardly part of this world - more like an onlooker. This nightmare went on throughout the year. Christmas 1982 passed, and my condition was no different. I had been prescribed a morphine-based tablet to suppress the pain, and I was to take hundreds of these over the duration of my illness. In early 1983 I decided to pay Bill a visit. It was then that he explained to me that a very real Satanic activity is the attempted destruction of anyone engaged in the ministry of Christian deliverance. This, he said, was especially true of those with new ministries and who were working alone. You will remember that I wrote about this at the beginning of the present chapter. My condition continued to deteriorate, and soon I could barely walk. At this point someone made us an offer for the watchglass side of our business, and we accepted a figure that was only a fraction of its real value. We agreed that he could pay us over a period of five years, interest free.

Our clergyman son, David, visited us on Easter Monday. Before he left, he prayed with me. He told me I must pray for life. The next day I had an unexpected experience. Late that morning, having washed and shaved, I was standing in front of my dressing table mirror, trying, with little success, to fasten my shirt collar buttons. Suddenly a dark cloud obscured my vision, and in the middle of it appeared a bright light. Then followed words, spoken into my mind, that said: "the Lord will heal his servant". Friends had never visited me - they somehow believed they must not do so. I had felt increasingly isolated and alone. June arrived, and with it my birthday. In no way was this an occasion for celebration. I felt almost dead.

Some two weeks later, shortly after lunch, I was standing in the hallway of my home. Looking into the wall-mirror, what I saw horrified me. On my face was the look I had seen so often some forty years before on the faces of Asian labourers on the Thailand-

Burma railway - a look that said that death was near. I hauled myself upstairs and collapsed onto my bed, filled with anger against God. In tears I shouted at him: "Just what are you doing? The last time I had dealings with you healed a child of leukaemia. What about me!"

I went downstairs and told Agnes what I had done. Then I was driven to my business to attend as best I could to any urgent jobs. Shortly after my arrival I received a 'phone call from a lady who wished to place an order for special glasses. She was a Christian, and she had promised six months earlier to visit me. She was to have brought with her a Christian man well-known for his healing ministry. Accepting her apology for not doing so, I told her what I had said to God an hour before.

A few minutes after I rang off I felt new life entering my body. It was as if I were being charged up from an unknown source. This continued during successive days, and within a week I was able to drive the car again. Not long afterwards I handed over the business to its new owner, and Agnes and I went on holiday for a week. On our return I visited the factory regularly for some three months, so that the takeover would be smooth and production uninterrupted. By now we had managed to sell the lease of our old factory. In doing so we had produced enough cash to pay off exactly our bank overdraft.

Although life had been given back to me and I was experiencing healing throughout my body, a further eighteen months was to pass before I was entirely free of pain. I am now completely well. Despite my advancing years my eyesight is excellent and my hands completely steady. I could, if necessary, carry out the most intricate of watch repair work. How thankful I am for my healing! Furthermore, throughout that strange and terrible illness, God had given me new insights into the spiritual battle. That he had been involved all along was revealed to me by the person whom I had come to value as my spiritual director. You will remember him as the clergyman to whom God had given the vision of his protecting angels around me. I met him shortly after my recovery.

Unexpectedly, he said to me: "I knew that God would not let you die, Jack." He meant that God had told him.

Yet I still ask the question: "Was Bill right? Did Satan and his demons really try to kill me?"

20

The light of Christ overcomes darkness in many

On hearing that I was in circulation again, friends in the watch repair wholesale trade promised me their immediate patronage should I become equipped to make special shaped watch-glasses. The replacement of broken ones was becoming a real problem for them. I soon developed a viable process, and found sources of diamond grinding wheels and thin glass necessary for doing the job. Gradually I found I could produce any shape of watch-glass and fit it to a watch case in an average time of fifteen minutes. This proved far more profitable than watch repair work. Just two days each week spent on watch-glass making produced all the money I needed.

Soon I found myself involved once more with people in spiritual darkness of various sorts. One person was a young doctor who had suffered recurrent depression since childhood and who had been a patient in various psychiatric hospitals for some years. The basic problem proved to be self-rejection. Happenings since his adoption in early childhood had reinforced the grip that this spirit had on his unconscious mind. After some six weeks of counselling and prayer the demonic hold appeared to have been broken, and the person quite soon began to enjoy an improved quality of life. Yet, as I will explain later, I now believe that complete exorcism of the self-rejection spirit had not been achieved. In this case, as in many others, the spiritual authority available to us through Jesus had driven out the darkness. The person remained free of depression for some years. Yet demonic forces can remain hidden deep within us, and their power can remain inactive, so long as we are walking "victoriously" in our Christian life. It is only when the opportunity arises (for example, in the case of self-rejection, the tragedy of another failed relationship) that the enemy is able to continue his work. Secrecy is part of Satan's battle plan. God needs every part of our soul to be laid bare to him if he is to be able to heal us. This he does through the searching work of the Holy Spirit in the context of pastoral counselling. The practical ministry which can then follow should bring complete deliverance from demonic forces.

During the 1980s the Bradford Diocesan Council of Healing held an annual weekend conference at a Christian centre in the Dales. It had been at one of these that I had come to know that my ministry was that of deliverance. It was there also that the remarkable vision about my protection from Satan had been given. At a conference held in the spring of 1985, some twenty of us were sharing what had been happening in our churches during the previous year. Towards the end of the discussion a lady called Betty, well-known for her charismatic leanings, asked the question, "Has anyone here got a bad shoulder?" She went on: "I've had this aching shoulder all the time we've been talking together, and it certainly is not mine!"

You will remember my account of the nightmare experience in which Satan had threatened to kill me, and of the awful things that had begun to happen afterwards? You will recall the occasion of that dark night when, blinded by the light of my son Philip's welding torch, I had fallen headlong from the raised drive in my garden onto the rockery three feet below. Although my head had missed the rocks, I had landed on my right shoulder. It had been wrenched almost out of its socket. As I said earlier, that shoulder was to become a source of trouble, and the pain was to worsen as time went on. Five years had passed and I was now almost unable to drive. I was having to think seriously of selling my beloved, but very heavy old car. The answer to my problem would lie in buying a smaller one which had power steering.

As soon as Betty had finished speaking, I enquired in which shoulder she had experienced the pain. "In my right one", she replied. In a couple of sentences I explained what had happened to me. Like lightning she was at my side, with a friend close on her heels! They immediately laid hands on my head, and began to pray for my healing. Normally, my reaction to this sort of thing would have been, "Here we go again! Betty never misses an opportunity!" Then they began to pray in tongues. However, instead of thinking, "They're over the top again!" I found myself thanking God for my healing, and was aware of a profound feeling of peace.

Physically, I felt absolutely nothing at the time. Yet when I began my journey home I realised that I had been healed. During the next few days I tackled a heavy engineering job without feeling any pain at all in my shoulder. It has remained strong and pain-free ever since. I had received that injury during a time of real spiritual conflict. God now reminded me that he is no man's debtor. Instead, when we suffer for Christ's sake, he always blesses us.

I kept my car for another year or so, and then decided to change it. I was fortunate to find a used vehicle in excellent condition. It was a large car, without power steering, made in Japan.

In my spiritual life also, there was some cleaning up to do. Again it was Betty who was the means of bringing some of this about. I bumped into her in a church one day, and she immediately drew me to one side. She told me that she believed God had told her that I must confess to Agnes a wrong relationship of many years before. I knew that she was referring to the person whose face had appeared to me in the dream in which Satan had said he would kill me. Betty knew nothing about it. Only God could have told her.

I made arrangements for Agnes and myself to visit our clergyman friend, Bill. I confessed the whole matter to Agnes in front of him. We were very conscious of the presence of Christ, and of his love surrounding us. Agnes not only forgave me, but my confession drew us even more closely together. I have since recognised that many Christians are fearful to confess unfaithfulness to their partners. They do not wish to hurt them, and fear losing them. Yet when the Holy Spirit leads us to bring such matters to God, forgiveness, reconciliation and peace always ensues. Satan's ground for accusation has been removed.

The events of the early 1980s had left me with two unrecognised problems - anger and self-condemnation. My peace of mind and heart, and the spiritual assurance received through Bill's ministry a few years before, had been partially lost. How easy it is in charismatic ministries to step out of the bounds of God's grace! Through a combination of our own fault and lack of support in our churches our spiritual integrity and security can be lost. My anger was revealed to me through a Christian friend. He had discerned it in my furious reply to a church member who had said that any belief today in supernatural healing and the like was absolute rubbish! I respected my friend's opinion, and prayed about it. Within a week I recognised in my heart that I had been guilty of spiritual pride. In my lone battle involving clergy at various levels I had been put down, not believed, and had received no recognition for anything I had done. At the same time, I had made mistakes. Through spiritual pride I had taken on ministry that had led me out of the bounds of God's grace. Then I had opened myself up, unknown to others, to a spirit of self-condemnation which had partially robbed me of my spiritual authority in Christ.

In my prayers I asked God what to do. Almost immediately he put his answer into my mind. He showed me that I needed to practise what I preached! That meant once again destroying the "self life", and being prepared to become "of no reputation". Christ himself had done that, and had been obedient to his Father. For him, it had meant facing death by crucifixion. Yet the outcome had been to receive from God all authority in heaven and earth. The message for me was clear. I immediately repented, and experienced a real sense of God's love.

Then I found myself recalling the verse at the beginning of Paul's letter to the Romans, Chapter 8. Here we read that there is no condemnation for those who are in Christ Jesus, because the law of the Spirit of life in Christ has freed us from the law of sin and death. It was as if God were saying to me, "You have believed wrongly that this verse means, as one redeemed through Christ, that you have been delivered from sin, and are forgiven by me. This is certainly true. Yet, through men, you have accepted condemnation in your heart. This itself is a sin, and you need to repent of it. For if I do not condemn you, you must on no account accept condemnation from anyone else on earth."

I remember that I was walking down my garden path when that message came to me. I acted upon it there and then. Immediately, the burden that had overshadowed me for a long time lifted away.

Soon I knew a new freedom, and the joy of my salvation was fully restored. I had experienced self-deliverance. This is something available to all of us when God truly reveals to us the nature of our sin and we are prepared to act on it.

At about this time, the then vicar of our church, who had succeeded Brandon Jackson fourteen years before, moved on to what might be his last ministry before retirement. Prior to his leaving, we had for two years been praying that our church might be renewed in the Holy Spirit. Each Saturday morning, church members who held that vision had met together at about 8.00 a.m. for a time of praise and intercession. For a good hour each week they had sought the anointing of the Spirit, that our church might receive an outpouring of his love, wisdom and power. Our vicar, who was a quiet man of great integrity, had suffered many spiritual buffetings during his years with us. Before he left, he had shared with some of us his beliefs about the future of the Anglican Church. He had become convinced that, unless it was renewed in the Holy Spirit, it would die. He did not mean that the Church as a whole needed to be wildly charismatic, placing undue emphasis on the

Gifts of the Holy Spirit. Our own church congregation was a large one, made up of young and old, with widely differing preferences in matters of liturgy and worship. Rather, he envisaged a Church that was spiritually alive, aware not only of what salvation in Christ really means, but knowing the reality also of the Church's involvement in the spiritual battle against evil. I believe that such change can take place within traditional, prayer-book based worship as well as within the modern, extravert, openly charismatic sort. What matters is that our faith and worship become real! Out of that reality will come freedom and ability to communicate our faith to others. It may well be that some traditional worshippers may be able to express themselves more freely in new ways. I know a clergyman who up to the age of fifty was a quiet, very knowledgeable, but rather ineffectual man. In no way could it be said that his ministry was powerful. Then he experienced spiritual renewal. I do not know whether or not this happened as a result of prayerful longing on his part. What I do know was that his preaching and personal ministry to others was transformed. However, his personality remained virtually the same. He was still quiet, yet had a new confidence and effectiveness that was evident to all. On some occasions I ministered to people with this man. We sometimes shared spontaneous prayer in tongues, something that would have been previously quite impossible to do.

During my lifetime in my own church, years of organised evangelism had succeeded little in bringing non-Christians to faith. The use of man's ways of communication - e.g. letters and tracts accompanying the parish magazine, invitations to social functions, special evangelistic church services - all had proved expensive in time and effort. They had been sadly ineffectual in winning people for Christ. If we are to be successful, our largely pagan society needs to be made conscious of a supernatural love and power in us - the result of a real relationship with God through Jesus. People need to perceive that real Christians are not people who use faith in God as a crutch in life. They need to know them as people with a real Jesus-like relationship with God, and who really know him as their source of blessing, guidance and protection. As in New Testament days, this change can only happen in us through a dynamic working of the Holy Spirit.

Fortunately for my church, our next vicar was able to build on our two years of prayer for renewal. For there had indeed begun a change amongst us. I had seen a lessening of the passivity that had brooded over our Sunday morning congregations for so long. Now I could actually see signs of life. Real praise - albeit subdued - was breaking out here and there! Our new leader was quietly charismatic, and had experienced a real call to evangelism and to the Christian healing ministry. He was in his early forties, and had a loving and positive personality which was a real blessing to me. We spent some time in conversation together during his first weeks with us. He was concerned about my spiritual health, and keen that I should be used quietly in the deliverance prayer ministry within his parish. From the outset I received his support and love. In return I was willing to come under his authority as well as that of the wider Church.

Fairly soon after his arrival my ministry took a new turn. This stemmed from a chance meeting with someone previously unknown to me. The Bradford Diocesan Council of Healing had ceased to exist as a separate entity, and had become part of the Church's healing ministry at Bradford Cathedral. I soon found myself completely occupied with people from within my own parish, and occasionally with the odd person from further afield. One afternoon, quite by accident, I met one such person at the house of an acquaintance. About forty years of age, she was in a most disturbed state. After several years of marriage, her husband had left her for someone else. She had found a new male companion, but the trouble was that her new partner was involved in witchcraft! He had soon grown tired of the relationship, and had finally rejected her. She had then started to explore the Christian faith. It was at this point that the woman began to experience torment and depression. Having shared these things with myself and my wife, she said she would like to discuss the matter further at some opportune time.

In fact, some months elapsed before she called on us. By this time she had formed a relationship with another man, somewhat younger than herself. She was also receiving counselling in the Christian faith from a female member of the church she now attended. Confusion was present through occult influence and because she was receiving unsound teaching. This I found hardly surprising when I discovered that her counsellor herself had a spiritual problem - something I will not speak of here. It did not take long to get our new friend's doctrine right. Within a few months this source of her confusion had been dealt with. Unfortunately, by that time I had discovered that her new partner and his family were all occultly subjected people! This discovery confirmed something I had come to believe with increasing certainty over the years. After the war, after receiving help from Bob, I had been quickly led to the spiritualist and his friends whose activities I had then decided to investigate in order to find out where my Christian beliefs fitted in. Since that time during my ministry there have been many occasions when it appeared that our enemy had led people from one situation of occult influence to another. in order that they might remain under bondage. Considering that the Bible speaks of the myriads of angels who are God's ministering spirits sent to serve those who are to obtain salvation (see Hebrews Ch1 v14), is it not logical to assume that the devil's angels will seek to do the opposite?

Over twelve months I remained alongside this lady (I will call her Barbara), dealing with the occult problem both in respect of herself and her new partner. The attachment, ostensibly a powerful bond of true love, proved to be nothing of the sort. The man was possessive, jealous and untrusting - and the love was counterfeit. They eventually separated and I persuaded Barbara to attend a different church from the one at which they were both members.

From this point on, things appeared to get better, but then took a new turn for the worse. Barbara became withdrawn and depressed. In my ministry to her there had been times when she had reacted very strangely, throwing her arms about in great distress. Had I been given more time, I believe that the problem would have been revealed to me. In the event, I had to discontinue helping her because my wife had to enter hospital for surgery. Although her operation was straightforward, it was to prevent me from engaging in ministry to people for several months. Some time after this, Barbara rang to ask if she might call on me again. She told me she had something very special to share.

Certainly, what she had to relate was very special. It was to bring that new dimension to my own ministry of which I hinted at the beginning of this story. As I listened to her, I soon realised that she was now a different person. Apparently, some time after she had stopped seeing me, she had accepted help from a man who possessed what I would describe as a direct deliverance ministry. This person (I will call him Mike) lived many miles away from her home. She had made several visits to his house to describe her background and give details of her life up to that time. Mike exercised a joint ministry with his wife.

He was quite clear as to his method of procedure and as to what he was about. He had come into this ministry of deliverance only a few years before. This had had been recognised by his church, which was a large, well established non-denominational one. His approach to deliverance was to free people from demonic subjection. At the outset he would explore every area of possible satanic attack or oppression in a person's life. This involved looking into occult, sexual, and rejection areas. Having recognised, through questioning and spiritual discernment by himself and his wife, areas that needed exploring - a process that could take several hours - he later would undertake what was, in effect, direct exorcism of evil spirits - the root causes of the person's problem.

Although Barbara explained to me what had happened to her, I do not think it right to relate to you what, after all, was a very private and confidential matter. I will instead tell you what happened when I allowed Mike to minister to me! This took place after I had visited him socially. Having heard much of my life story, he had discerned that there were certain things to be dealt with. I was quite happy to let him deal with them, especially if, in the end, it would strengthen my own ministry. His method of procedure was, after all, different from mine. With my vicar's consent, I fixed an appointment for some weeks ahead. After two visits during which he questioned me for a total of four hours, we agreed a date on which he would start his deliverance prayers. He had asked me to fast as much as possible during the previous twenty-four hours. Once at his house, he asked me to sit in an upright chair in the centre of the room. His wife was present, and he first spent some time in prayer. He explained that he was firstly to deal with rejection, and "fruits" of rejection. These were themselves minor spirits, which stemmed from the root of rejection. Having repeated after him a prayer of renunciation, he began his ministry to me. Having placed one hand on my head and the other over my solar plexus, and addressed the spirit, telling it to manifest and come out!

He had already explained that, during his time of ministry, spirits would show their presence physically, sometimes making a person feel sick, or retch, cough or yawn deeply, according to the type of spirit commanded to leave. I had read in many books that this was supposed to happen, but had never yet experienced it myself. He asked me to help this process of exorcism by coughing, which apparently would often trigger off actual release and expulsion of the spirits through the mouth. On a table at his side were the notes made during my interviews, and any spirits that might possibly be present were to be confronted, one by one. In due course he explored the occult and sexual realms. I was very aware of the Spirit's presence. Yet the presence of his hands on my head and solar plexus seemed to make it difficult for me to think clearly. I did as requested, and I coughed - sometimes more spontaneously than at others - and I would often yawn. Yet I was under strain and getting tired. I occasionally had tingling in my fingers, and tightness in my head. The possibility of these having a spiritual source was taken seriously, and commands to leave continued to be addressed to the spirit being dealt with at the time, until the sensations had ceased.

It may well be that the hours spent with me had been far more effective than I imagined. Certainly, my confidence in my own spiritual authority began gradually to improve during the following months. However, there was one time during his ministry to me when a spirit definitely did manifest, and this gave me a valuable

161

insight into our enemy's ways. The spirit Mike was addressing was "unforgiveness". In the middle of his authoritative prayers I heard a voice speak into my mind which said, mockingly, "I'm the one you should be after, not that!" At the same time, I was aware of my eyes changing and taking on a mocking look, and of my head turning to the left to conceal what was a mocking smile. I was petrified. All this did not go unnoticed, and was dealt with.

Immediately, I knew the source of this spirit. You will recall the lady I met shortly after I found myself being involved in spiritual warfare -I first met her whilst speaking to a group that was preparing for confirmation. I met her again when I was asked by a clergyman friend to help him with a case of "possession". You may remember that when the woman was dealt with later by the Bishop's Chaplain for Exorcism, it had come to light that she had been involved with all types of occult practices, including witchcraft. I believe I received considerable spiritual damage from that woman. At that time I was not sufficiently knowledgeable or spiritually equipped to deal with such evil things.

Towards the end of our time with this person, my friend and I, in our ignorance, had begun to pray for healing. The woman was seated, and I was standing close behind her. She must have been unaware that I, looking down, could see her face. Suddenly her eyes changed to those of a witch, and a horrifying, mocking smile formed on her mouth. I remember the terrible stab of fear that hit my solar plexus. There is no doubt in my mind now that a spirit of mockery entered at that point.

This confirmed my previous belief that it is possible for an evil spirit to reside within Christians. Yet if we really lead righteous lives it will not be able to manifest itself through us. There is no way in which I, over the years, have mocked people, even in argument. Yet this spirit must have been within me for more than twenty years. Since this very surprising revelation took place I have recognised the same situation in other people. I know a lovely middle-aged lady who is classed medically as a manic-depressive. In her times of depression all her spiritual values turn upside down, and her reasoning base becomes grossly distorted. Since she has become a "born-again" Christian her attacks have occurred only infrequently. The fact that her elderly mother is a medium I believe is not without significance! I am confident that she could, through exorcism, be freed from what is really a spiritual problem. Yet unless she actually seeks spiritual help she will continue to remain in bondage.

Following upon my ministry from Mike, two other friends in whom I had confided sought his help also. They were not members of my church, and they lived many miles away from me. They had felt intuitively that they could benefit from Mike's ministry. In fact, they both obtained release from spiritual damage received over many years. As in Barbara's case, demons had apparently been expelled as a result of direct prayers of authority which had been undertaken after a long period of preparation and counselling.

After my own experience of Mike's ministry, and having seen the dramatic and obvious benefits experienced by my friends, I found myself pondering the subject of the exorcism of demons. If the matter was as real as it seemed, should I not myself be able to exercise this more direct ministry? Many people who had sought help from me over the years had appeared to be demonised. Yet, hitherto, I had been warned and more or less forbidden by the Church against going down this road. In ministering to a person, my approach had been firstly to acquire knowledge of all the facts relevant to the case and then gently but authoritatively to pray into the situation. Having, by the Holy Spirit's leading, through confession, uncovered the causes of the problem, I would pray as required. Often this would mean bringing the person to true repentance, and a real experience of God's forgiveness. Then I would quietly but firmly take authority over the evil spirits and deny them power to work in the person's life. Only once, as a result of such prayers, had the release been dramatic. On that occasion a spirit of fear had appeared to leave by the mouth. More often, the Holy Spirit had worked without much apparent activity from me. I decided to pray hard about this whole matter.

I have already emphasized many times that I have learnt from experience never to offer direct help to people, having found that the Spirit leads to us those for whom God has plans. Equally, in this matter of direct exorcism, I decided not to enter this area out of curiosity or a desire to "test the water". Yet, remarkably, some months later my prayers were answered in a way that precluded any temptation to take such a course of action.

I received a telephone call from the two friends in whom I had confided about Mike's special ministry and whom he had later helped. Although they lived in Lancashire, some two hours drive from my home, they pressed me to pay them a visit as soon as ever possible. They wished to introduce me to a young man they were very anxious to help. My wife and I arrived at their house early one Friday evening, having arranged to stay overnight. The young man (I will call him Tony) arrived by car at about seven-thirty. He was about twenty-five, and attended the same church as my friends. In early life he had been subjected to violence over a long period, and some months before our meeting he had been attacked and raped by three men. Now he was agoraphobic, full of fear, and terribly depressed. His personality had not developed beyond that of a fourteen-year-old. After only a short conversation with Tony, my friends asked me to help him there and then. I realised that they had "set me up"! They had arranged this meeting so that I would not only get acquainted with this young man, but so that I could, hopefully, minister to him!

I walked across the room from where I had been sitting next to my wife and drew up a chair close to Tony. Before I had said a word he began to tremble from head to foot. I recognised this as the activity of a spirit of fear at work in him. I found myself immediately addressing this spirit, quietly and firmly binding its power over him. I talked to him for some time, gently and lovingly assuring him that all was under control. I asked him to tell me briefly about his awful experiences. At this point he burst into tears, clinging hold of me.

One thing of which I have become certain over recent years is that when a person suffers violent assault, either physically or sexually, or both, the terrible fear engendered in the person at the time allows unclean spirits to enter. In the case of sexual assault I

164

have known several cases where unclean, sex-related spirits, as well as spirits of fear and terror, have affected the person's behaviour and personality for years afterwards. I would go as far as to say that such damage will remain unless these spirits are expelled through exorcism.

When Tony had calmed down somewhat, I decided to minister to him, and addressed directly the unclean spirits that I discerned were present. Almost immediately, Tony doubled in half and started to retch. Over the next half hour several spirits were expelled, after which Tony felt very weak.

My wife and I returned home next day. Only a week or two elapsed before our friends were able to tell us that Tony's agoraphobia and fear had disappeared. They too got alongside this young man and helped build up his faith. Later, they themselves were to be drawn into the deliverance ministry. They had seen the reality of demonic subjection in the life not of someone unknown to them, but present in a Christian in their own church. The tragedy there, as in so many churches today, was that clergy and church leaders had no experience or awareness of any ministry of deliverance. They gave scant credance to any nonsensical belief that Satan might still be active today - especially within the Church!

Tony was to be the first of several people to be released in a similar way over the following months. The remarkable thing was that in some cases the person concerned would recognise that such ministry was required, and would then ask me to carry it out! One person was a very gentle lady in her early fifties who had been depressed since she was sixteen. I spelt out to her some nineteen fruits of self-rejection, and she was able to identify with them all, so that I became certain that such a spirit was at work. She had no problem about letting me minister to her, and the results were quite dramatic. An interesting fact concerning this case was that there was no reaction to my prayers of authority for a full five minutes. Demons do not want to reveal themselves! Then the woman, trembling all over, began to retch and yawn. After some fifteen minutes she calmed down and regained her composure. Together with my female assistant I then prayed with her and gave control of her life to Jesus Christ. We continued alongside her for several weeks, by which time she had become a quietly self-confident person. She had been freed from the "endogenous depression" - her psychiatrist's diagnosis - which had kept her in darkness for so many years!

Finally, I will give accounts of the deliverance of three men, whose problems differed radically from each other, requiring different types of ministry.

I have been friends with Ken for many years. He is of Scots descent and has a wry sense of humour. As a Christian, working as chief accountant for a large manufacturing firm, he had gone through hard times in an effort to maintain his Christian standards. Living some distance from me, he worshipped at my church whenever he could. One morning, at the end of a service of Holy Communion, he appeared at the entrance to the side-chapel where I and others had been helping someone who had asked for prayer. A mutual friend had brought Ken to me. He was extremely upset and in tears. He told us that his brother, a chronic depressive, was in a suicidal state and was locked in a padded room in a psychiatric hospital in Glasgow.

That was all he told me. Still standing there together, I prayed a short prayer. In it told the suicidal spirit to leave, and asked the Lord for his protection. Then we went home.

Ten days later I met Ken at a friend's house. I suddenly remembered our last meeting.

"How is your brother?", I asked.

"You should know", he replied. "At the exact time of our prayer he was freed from his depression. At present he is quite well and in Florida!"

Here was another example of someone into whose life the Holy Spirit had temporarily intervened and had driven out darkness. The main work now lay ahead - that of discerning the cause of his chronic problem, dealing with it, and then introducing him to the

Christian life. Unfortunately we did not have opportunity to do this, and a year or two later he died suddenly from a physical illness.

My second story is entirely different from the one above. In fact, it has quite a humorous side to it.

One day I received a phone call from a woman who was involved in counselling within a nearby parish. I knew this person and had worked with her a few times. Would I, she asked, be prepared to talk to a male associate from work whose wife had deep spiritual problems? I told her to bring him along the following lunchtime. They arrived at my house the next day at about 2.00 p.m. The man was in his early forties. Over a cup of tea, I asked him to explain his wife's problem. He told me that she had been introduced to a group of charismatic Christians who seemed to be full of the Holy Spirit, and she wanted to be like them. The trouble was, he said, that she would not let them touch her or pray with her. She wanted to find God for herself, apparently. Because her behaviour was so much out of character he had decided to move out and live with his brother for the time being.

There was no means of my knowing the truth of what he had said, but in the end it was seen to have no relevance to the man's real problem. For, suddenly, out of the blue he said to me: "It's really me who needs the help!" He began to recount an amazing story. Apparently, when he was about fourteen, he had been at a party and had met a girl a bit older than himself who had made amorous approaches to him - probably kissing him, I suspect, as he retreated backwards in an attempt to evade her. Soon he found himself trapped against a hot radiator. It was then that he "felt something happen" - a sort of sexual arousal.

Once he had reached teenage he began to experience lustful feelings regularly, and since then had been involved sexually with many women. The strange thing, however, was that he was sexually aroused by hot radiators! This, I thought, was the ultimate in conditioned reflexes! I realised that he needed deliverance from the lustful spirit he had received from the girl at the party. I invited him to see me again the very next day

The couple arrived next day at lunchtime, as promised. As is often the case with severely demonised persons, the man reacted to exorcism immediately. It is often the case where spirits of lust or uncleanness are present, that retching begins straight away. Typically, the man felt the source of the problem to be in his solar plexus area, moving eventually upwards into his chest. Although the retching was prolonged, not much sputum was discharged into the receptacle we had provided. The mystery is that demons appear to leave in a physical way, sometimes with foul smells, coughing, yawning etc, but, of course, they are in reality spiritual forces or entities not normally seen with the human eye. However, I have studied writings of deeply spiritual people - including well-known persons - who record having "seen" demons leave people, or inhabit places, whilst engaged in ministry under the power of the Holy Spirit.

In this case, the actual exorcism lasted only a few minutes, after which the man felt at peace, though physically shattered. This is often the case after demonic life has been driven out of people. Finally, I prayed with him and then asked the couple to visit me again in a week's time. At that meeting the man told me that he now felt to be a new person - "clean inside". Then he confessed an illegitimate affair he was having when he first came to see me! He had repented of this and broken off the relationship.

The last time I heard of this man he was still at peace and attempting to lead the Christian life. He had been in spiritual bondage to this uncleanness for over twenty years! To remain free he would need to spend much time amongst those who would nurture him in the Christian faith. His spiritual cleansing would be helped by taking Holy Communion regularly, and by receiving prayer ministry with spiritually equipped people. This would need to continue until he reached the point at which he was able completely to resist any temptation to revert to his former way of life.

You will read in many books on deliverance that people who insist that they are demonised rarely are, and there is certainly truth in that statement. Yet I believe we must treat every case individually, and learn to discern for ourselves, under the guidance of the Holy Spirit, what is the truth in each case. I could fill many pages with accounts of deliverance and of ministry to people in spiritual darkness. Each case would continue my attempt to convince the reader of the sinister reality of the spiritual battle, a battle that exists today just as it did in the time of St. Paul. His advice given then in his letter to the Church at Ephesus was never more relevant than it is today. My desire and longing has been, and always will be, to bring people out of darkness into the glorious light of Christ. How could I express better my thanks to God for my own protection and deliverance over so many years? In exchange, I have received from him an overflowing, inexpressible joy whenever those bound in spiritual darkness have been set free by his holiness and power. Then I am filled with wonder, love and praise for the God and Father of us all, who has granted to us every spiritual blessing through Jesus Christ our Lord.

Finally, I will tell you of a deliverance that took place only shortly before I began to write this book. It is one that demonstrates very well the way in which the Holy Spirit can first bring a person out of spiritual darkness and torment and then use him to help others. As in the case of the child who was dying of leukaemia, the Holy Spirit used others besides myself as agents of his work.

For several years, whenever possible, a good number of men of my church attended a monthly "Men's Breakfast". Organised by a small committee, men were encouraged to bring non-Christian friends to a Saturday morning meeting held at a local riverside restaurant. It started at 8:30 a.m. and finished round about ten o' clock. It was a happy event - evangelistic in purpose. At the tables during breakfast there was opportunity for fellowship, discussion, and talk about sport and other things. As was usual on these occasions the meeting proper began with a testimony by someone. This could be an account of how the person had become a Christian, or of how God appeared to be doing something remarkable in a person's life. This was usually followed by an exposition of a portion of Scripture, undertaken by someone who had a real gift of bringing the Bible to life for us.

For about four years a certain gentleman had regularly attended these meetings without ever becoming a true Christian. On the day of the story I am about to tell he did something he had done regularly over those years - interrupt the proceedings! At this point I had something to say about the man's problem, something I had discerned about him but will not mention here. In the event, some of the men present could not get their head around what I had said - a sad comment on their lack of understanding or discernment of deep spiritual things! Sadly, that was to be expected, for in common with most churches, there never had been teaching in our church about profound spiritual matters involved in the battle between good and evil.

When the meeting ended I was the last to leave. Outside the door a young man was waiting. He was in tears, and obviously distressed. "You can help me!", he said.

I led him away from the restaurant to a quiet spot. There, after saying a short prayer with him, I invited him to visit me at home on the following Monday evening

This young man (I will call him Martin) was in his early twenties, and his lovely young wife was expecting their first baby. He arrived at my home as arranged, and without delay began to pour out his problem - or what really were the symptoms of his problem. I listened to him for a long time. From the outset, he appeared to trust me and to know that I had a real desire to help him. He was depressed, confused and in a state of inner torment that I had seen in others so many times before. It did not take long to identify the causes of his condition.

He had consulted his doctor, who had prescribed anti-depressant drugs. As in all such cases, these only address the symptoms, and not the causes, of a person's condition. At best, they can only give a little respite from the inner suffering being experienced by, if you like, anaesthetising them against it. Then, perhaps, they may regain some strength. Yet eventually there can be a price to pay in the form of unpleasant, sometimes severe, withdrawal symptoms.

Martin then told me something which he had, no doubt, kept to himself for years. As a child he had been sent to boarding school. At age fifteen, and still not interested in girls, he had been accused by some of his fellow students of being a homosexual. He had taken this on board and it had worried him ever since.

Then he told me he was practising homeopathy, a subject about which most people are quite ignorant. Unaware of its origins, Martin, like many others, was easily persuaded to try it as a means of healing

Homeopathy was founded in 1810 by Hahnemann, whose understanding of spirit was "vital energy" - the Hindu "prana" He was a Freethinker and a Freemason. He practiced Mesmerism - hypnotism based on occult power. Homeopathic preparations, diluted and shaken, are supposed to induce the "healing energy". Further dilutions, in the ratio of 100 - 1 are supposed to increase the power. This process is called "dynamisation". Repeated dilutions, followed by shaking, supposedly increases and retains the power in the liquid, its non-material essence. Homeopathy is dangerous because it operates through occult forces unwittingly invited in by those who submit to it.

Christians who do submit to it will experience a loss of reality of faith in Christ, and may fall into depression. The spirit behind homeopathy seduces the intellect into accepting the irrationality of its methods. The "prana" force comes straight out of Hinduistic teaching, with its many gods and belief in reincarnation. It has nothing to do with the Holy Spirit of Truth proclaimed by Christ, who declared that he himself was the Way, the Truth and the Life and that no-one could come to have a relationship with God except through him. Very dogmatic, but known to be true in the hearts of millions! Although the "prana"' force works when fully accepted, it does so at the expense of mankind's salvation in Christ.

If we look into the Old Testament, at Deuteronomy Chapter 18, verses 9 to 13, God spells out to the Israelites the dangers of engaging in any of the occult practices found in Canaan, when they came to enter that land which he had promised them so many years before. The things I have written about above, coupled with things like mediumism, necromancy (seeking to contact the dead), divination and all occult practices are here condemned as an abomination to God! Therefore, anyone who does practise them comes under God's curse, not his blessing.

Imagine my reaction, then, when Martin told me that his mother was a spiritualist medium!

The job of bringing deliverance to Martin did not involve any direct exorcism, because this young man was not demonised. Rather, he was, among other things, under severe spiritual oppression. Here was an intelligent young person, seeking to lead a normal life, but who was at the receiving end of various evil, spiritual forces. The great thing about him, as far as I was concerned, was his willingness to believe that what I was telling and teaching him was true, and to act upon it. The ability to do this was, I am certain, due to the convicting work of the Holy Spirit. The forces of spiritual oppression did not proceed from the medication he had been prescribed, but rather from the other sources mentioned earlier.

The accusation that Martin was a homosexual was not founded in fact. Yet if it were only partially believed, it would be able to induce fear of a subtle kind that would remain in his unconscious until dealt with. Such a spirit of fear can have an unrecognised, yet paralysing effect. In dealing with this I taught Martin, from Scripture, of God's love for him. I taught him also about the lies of our enemy, and prayed into the whole situation. The time came when Martin, by knowing the truth, was able to be completely free of what might have once seemed to him a curse, but which in reality had no grounds to stand on. There was no longer any power in the memory of that accusation to hurt him. Through the help of the Spirit and the Word of God he had received deliverance - the Truth had indeed set him free!

Before I had undertaken any of the previous ministry, I had confronted the major problem of Martin's mother being a medium. I had prayed prayers of protection for Martin and given the whole matter to God. Only now that Martin had been set free, and had given his whole life to Jesus Christ, was I in a position to loose him from the occult tie that had existed between himself and his mother. Only now could this happen, because "loosing" and "binding" of spiritual powers is not the simple matter often believed by some Christians. This is partly due to a mistranslation in some Bible versions of that portion of Scripture where Jesus speaks about these things. In Matthew 16, at verse 19, what the Greek really says is: "Whatever you bind on earth, having been bound in heaven, shall be: and whatever you loose on earth, having been loosed in heaven, shall be." In other words, only God, by his Spirit, binds evil spiritual forces, or looses us from them. Just claiming the words, without the presence of the Spirit's authority, will not do. In the case of Martin, because of the strength of his new-found faith and utter commitment to Christ, the way was open for me to pray with certainty.

Shortly after that God played a naughty joke. Because my wife had begun a long stay in hospital because of a heart infection, I was unable to attend further Men's Breakfasts. The six weeks of ministry had bridged a holiday period. One day, Martin was approached to give a testimony at the next breakfast meeting. He agreed to do so, and apparently it was quite something! He spoke about God transforming his life. The following day at church, knowing nothing of this, I couldn't fail to miss the stares of a couple of the Men's Breakfast leaders. They looked at me as if I were God! Yes, it was God, but not me. I was only doing what the Church should be doing for countless others. You see, I can never thank God enough for bringing me out of what was terrible darkness into the glorious light of Christ. Furthermore, I have discovered that God always vindicates those who love him.

The Holy Spirit had first worked in Martin through an acquaintance who had invited him to that breakfast meeting.

Strangely, this was the same person who had invited the man who had attended the meetings for four years without coming to faith. Later, Martin and his wife and baby became members of a local Baptist church. Younger friends of mine from my church got alongside them and they still remain friends. I heard that Martin changed jobs to take up paid Christian work for the poor.

21

Insights for those who minister to others

The story of my 'double journey" through life is virtually complete. You will have seen that the two strands of my narrative - the material and the spiritual - ran side by side for many years. At the outset I was ambitious and lived for my work. Eventually the two strands separated and the spiritual became all-important.

Maybe you decided to read this book because you were interested in learning of my experiences as a Japanese prisoner-of-war. Perhaps the unusual content of my story has retained your interest until now. If at the beginning you were unsure about Christianity, I would like to think that what you have read has enabled you to recognise the truth of Christ's Gospel. I hope and pray that you may come to embrace the faith - as in my case, that could be a life-changing experience.

In this last chapter I wish to share, with Christians who minister to others, some spiritual insights received over many years in the deliverance ministry.

Because our spirit is that part of us which communicates with God it is necessary, as I have said before, to develop the intuitive life. We must listen to God, one might say, with the 'ears of our spirit'. Knowledge from God received into our spirit is direct and not reasoned. In that sense it may be termed "supernatural". St. Paul, in his second letter to the Corinthian Church, wrote: "We have not received this world's spirit, instead, we have received the Spirit sent by God, that we may know all that God has given us." Thus, the ability to receive direct knowledge from God's Spirit when we are in a counselling or ministering situation is a priceless asset, and one that is unavailable to the secular counsellor. For "There is nothing that can be hidden from God; everything in all creation is exposed and lies open before his eyes." (Hebrews 4, v.13 Good News Bible (G.N.B.)). The Spirit works not only in the one being counselled, bringing to the consciousness hidden hurts or sins, but He also bestows relevant information 'supernaturally" to the Christian counsellor and minister.

I now want to share an insight that has impressed itself more and more on my consciousness as the years have gone by. Some may consider it to be self-evident; others may find it hard to accept. However, I will try to show from Scripture and from my own experience the validity of this concept. When applied, I believe it to be an invaluable help to those involved in the ministries of inner healing and deliverance, It may be summed up in the statement:

"Mind does not exist in isolation from spirit, but reflects our spirit's nature."

Because I am using my intellect (the reasoning part of my mind) as I write this, it would be foolish of me to try to prove that statement intellectually. The complex nature of mind in all its aspects and functions cannot be understood by us - mind cannot understand mind. We cannot understand the nature of thought, reasoning, memory, consciousness, imagination, truth and error, conjecture, etc. Therefore, I shall put them aside. In trying to validate my concept I will rely on Scripture and corroborative proof obtained in my own experience with those who have sought my help.

In the first letter of John, Chapter 2, we read at verse 27: "The anointing (by God's Spirit) which you received from him (through Christ) abides in you, and you have no need that anyone should teach you; as his anointing teaches you about everything, and is true and is no lie, just as it has taught you, abide in him." We see here that the Holy Spirit brings the mind of God to teach and direct us. Again, in 1 Corinthians, Chapter 2, vv 15, 16, we have: "The spiritual man judges all things, but is himself to be judged by no-one. "For who has known the mind of the Lord so as to instruct him? But we have the mind of Christ." In the letter to the Ephesians, Ch.4, vv 22, 23 we read: "Put off your old nature which belongs to your former manner of life and is corrupt through deceitful lusts, and be renewed in the spirit of your minds". Paul, throughout the New Testament, is continually exhorting us to use our wills to bring our minds into line with God's mind, as in Philippians Ch. 2, v 5: "Have this mind (or attitude) among yourselves, as was also in Christ Jesus, etc". It was the spiritual attribute of Christ's mind, his humility, coupled with his obedience to his Father, that enabled him to pay the price for our sins on the cross. In his letter to the Romans, Ch. 6, Paul spells out what really being "in Christ" is all about. The old nature in us needs to be destroyed by our being 'baptised into his death'. Only then, Paul tells us, are we raised with him into new life - his resurrection life. Again, in Romans Ch.12, v 2, Paul says: "Do not be conformed to this world, but be transformed by the renewal of your mind, that you may prove what is the will of God, what is good and acceptable and perfect." The Greek word for 'transformed' here is the word used by Mark for 'transfigured' when writing of Jesus' experience on the mountain with Peter, James and John. (Mark Ch. 9, v. 2) God desires our minds to be 'glorified' - to be as near as possible like his. This must particularly apply to those who are ministering to others.

So what of the spirits and minds of those whom we are called to counsel? Our clients' need for ministry is plain evidence of their more than average imperfection. Because good and evil are absolute values, the causes of spiritual ill-health are patently evil. This may appear a stark statement, and may seem so because we are used to rationalising and intellectualising our condition. The truth is that the things of spirit and mind are either of God or of Satan - there is no middle ground. Satan would persuade us otherwise. The Christian counsellor with the gift of discernment of spirits will not be deceived. He will not need to use clever body language, designed to conceal from the one being counselled his true feelings and reactions. Neither will he need to probe for 'hidden agendas' in an attempt to diagnose causes. The intuitive, discerning Christian, concealing nothing, but under the guidance of the Spirit of Truth, will rapidly uncover the activity of evil spirits where they lie at the root of the person's problem. Even if such activity is of a minor nature, it can, nevertheless, be discerned. It will manifest in three ways: (1) through bodily behaviour - eyes, facial expression, agitation, trembling, etc. (2) in the person's spirit, its nature being recognised through the gift of discernment of spirits, and (3) from the mind of the person, by the things he says. Let us take a few examples. Someone who is in the grip of a jealous spirit and who, say, is extremely jealous of a friend's attachment to someone else, will manifest this physically through the eyes (the 'green eye') and by a clinging, abnormal possessiveness towards his friend. Jealousy is a most obvious spiritual evil, easy to discern. A person who is led by the Holy Spirit can readily sense this spirit in a person. I have met it many times, and it can be a sickening experience. The jealousy is expressed outwardly in what the person says and in the tone of voice used. Denigration and rejection of the object of the jealousy become the continual topic of conversation, which is symptomatic of the person's inward condition.

Again, a spirit of fear is fairly easily diagnosed by the spiritual counsellor. Unease, "butterflies in the stomach", and trembling are just some of the physical symptoms experienced as the body reacts to an unseen but real aggressor. The fact that the fear may not be consciously recognised will produce a depression characterised by a thought life centred around situations generated by that spirit of fear. Conversation may be neurotic and demeanour apprehensive. Some years ago a young mother was brought to me who exhibited all these symptoms, but there was one other, over-riding symptom. She was constantly preoccupied with the thought that she might never recover from her depression, the cause of which she was unable to identify. She had received medical help and psychotherapeutic counselling over a long period, without result. Other Christians had been reluctant and even frightened to deal with her. They sensed something about her that was too deep for them to handle - reactions which made me suspect a spiritual cause. My suspicions were confirmed when I prayed with her toward the end of our first meeting. In what I call a "test prayer" - a general prayer in the middle of which I take authority over the evil one (in a non-frightening way) - there was a decided reaction. Within a matter of days I discerned that a spirit of fear had entered via a psychological route (something I will mention later), namely, it had entered via the mind. Only a short time later, with her husband present, did she experience a classic deliverance from the evil spirit - it left through the mouth.

As a third example, let us consider bitterness. This corrosive spiritual evil is closely related to hatred. Bitterness is generated by an unloving, unforgiving sour spirit, the physical effects of which are seen in the eventual development of a hard, unsmiling facial expression. This spirit may in time cause the facial muscles to grow in such a way as to make that grim expression permanent! This spirit in a person can be sensed by the hard, cold voice used to express thoughts which reflect the unforgiving, soured mind. Unforgiveness springs not from love, but from hatred. The Bible speaks of a "root of bitterness" that might spring up and defile us, thereby strangling spiritual growth. Many peripheral evils have the same source - things like criticism, a sneering manner, or a despising attitude. It is fairly easy to recognise a bitter person from the personality, the eyes, features and tone of voice. Most of all it is seen in what proceeds from the mind. Here again we have evidence of the link between mind and spirit, as the person pours out accusations against those who have hurt him. In some cases the hurts are so deep that any idea of forgiveness cannot be entertained. Yet the charismatically equipped counsellor is able, in the context of God's love and in the active power of the Holy Spirit, to reveal to the hurting person the true nature of his condition and to convince him of his need to forgive as the only means of deliverance and healing. The way becomes open when the Spirit succeeds in convicting and convincing him (dual work of God's Spirit and mind) of the truth of the counsellor's words. Unfortunately, many bitter people continue in their sad state for years without receiving effective help. Christians, especially, put on a cheerful face and profess unwavering faith. As their thoughts and emotions become repressed and hidden from consciousness, physical systemic problems may begin - psychosomatic illness. Unrecognised, the evil spirit still continues his destructive work.

There are evil forces which can operate in otherwise wholesome people. Being different in nature from a spirit of unforgiveness, they differ also in their effects. For example, a person who has a disdainful spirit can make life miserable both for himself and others. One who is oppressed by such a spirit has the false belief that those who are culturally, academically or in any other way inferior to him are unworthy, and to be despised. This makes him unable to feel at ease with such people or to communicate easily with them, and they in turn, feel unable to be relaxed or natural with him. The thoughts, attitudes and utterances generated by a disdainful spirit are responsible for this state of affairs. The above description sums up, perhaps, what may be described as "the snob syndrome". It is very difficult to find opportunity to free such people from this very real bondage. If we attempt to do so without the leading of the Holy Spirit we are liable to inflict hurt, create offence or enter into argument - another subtle trap of the enemy.

As I continue to examine this relationship between mind and spirit let me show, as promised earlier, how spiritual bondage can reach us through psychological channels. I will begin by relating a good example of this.

Some years ago a single young lady sought my help through a friend. She was in a severe state of depression, and had been in this condition for over two years. Her job on the production line of a printing works was a repetitive one. She was not very bright academically, neither was she good-looking. However, she was very good at her job and her production rate was above average. Her immediate boss, however, continually "put her down". He never gave her a word of praise or encouragement. Instead, the message she received every day in her dealings with him was that she was inferior to all her work-mates. It soon became clear to me that a spirit of self-rejection was at work in her. Her self-image was poor, she felt worthless, and she accepted completely her boss's message as true. I was able to help this lady only partially, since she remained trapped in the situation because she was financially dependent on her job. She has continued to struggle on, and has decided that her problem is a cross she must bear. Meanwhile, a degree of depression remains permanent, spoiling her whole existence.

I am sure that you will be able to think up for yourself many ways in which the mind can be the vehicle that enables spiritual oppression to gain a hold on us. A lustful spirit can grow strong in a person if, by act of will, he or she watches "blue" videos and reads pornographic magazines on a regular basis. Yet the secular world denies this. I once listened to a radio programme on which this subject was debated. One woman speaker rejected outright the possibility that pornography could influence its readers adversely. It could, she said, act as an outlet for frustrated desire in men. She also suggested that masturbation was a healthy activity for such people. Whilst disagreeing with her views, other speakers agreed that there was no evidence available that could disprove what she had said. The increased incidence of child abuse and rape they explained away. Those things had always been there, they insisted. Now they were being uncovered. What was needed, they said, was more money to be made available to our police forces. Not once was the subject of good and evil mentioned. There was no talk of God, Christianity, or morality, or even of a preference for a wholesome way of life. I found this discussion to be one more proof of the extent to which our secular society had become divorced from any understanding of mankind's spiritual nature.

I have a concept to put to you about which I hesitate to be dogmatic. It concerns our emotions. For years I have found it difficult to accept the way in which the emotions are dealt with by some psychiatrists, psychotherapists and others. These people consider the emotions to be something in themselves - a separate part of us, just as a leg or an arm is a separate member of our body. We hear references to our "emotional self", to the "healing of the emotions", and to the "the distortion of the emotions". Our soul, they say, consists of our emotions, intellect and will. Yet to me it is clear that these things are a function of the soul, which is that part of

181

us which is conscious of self. My experience shows me that our emotions (or lack of them) are responses or reactions to happenings or to information that has reached us. These may be either good or bad, and reach us either from the world outside or from within ourselves as the mind recalls those things. Our memories of traumatic, perhaps horrific incidents, can bring with them their related spiritual forces. They may even cause a re-living of the event in nightmares. Over the years since the war, I have been deeply saddened on many occasions to hear of ex-Far East P.O.W.s who continue to experience such nightmares and whose lives are clouded by depression. In these situations, where the damage is in the deep mind of the spirit, deliverance and healing can only be found through ministry in the power of God's Holy Spirit. This alone can dissolve away what is unreachable by psychiatrists, who may know or discover the causes of a person's condition, but are unable to remove the spiritual force that created it.

On receiving good news we experience elation, and when confronted by danger we experience fear. The sight of a child being knocked down and killed before our eyes can fill us with horror. The sight of a child being cruelly beaten will fill us with anger. It is possible to experience a multitude of emotions - envy, jealousy, pity, sorrow, delight, excitement, despair, self-pity etc., etc. We "feel" them in our being, via our nervous system. Chemical reactions take place in our bodies which differ according to the emotion experienced. Fear releases adrenalin to increase the level of sugar in our bloodstream, thereby enabling us to flee. Note, however, that all these emotions have spiritual names. If an emotional reaction takes place suddenly, it is virtually a reflex, by-passing our will - as in the case of sudden anger in a situation. Our will usually regains control in time to prevent us expressing our anger by violent means. We can be filled with anger in response to thoughts about a person or a past situation - anger that can come and go as our thoughts subside. We experience "emotion" when spiritual energy, aroused in the various ways mentioned, breaks into our consciousness. Soulish people will enjoy the emotional life for its own sake. They will seek artificially to arouse their feelings in various ways. The huge crowds that flock to festivals of popular music - particularly rock music - are doing exactly that. Yet it is possible for Christians to do the same. I can think of one or two well-known U.S. evangelists who appeal to our self-indulgence via emotionalism, and that has very little to do with the real activity of the Holy Spirit. This may even apply to our church services. Yet when the Spirit triggers our emotions, they are of the highest order. When Mary knew she was to be the mother of Jesus she said: "My soul magnifies (praises) the Lord, and my spirit rejoices in God my Saviour." Her whole being looked toward God. Similarly today, when Christians are truly praising God in the Spirit, they may find themselves with hands spontaneously raised in the air. This is entirely different in nature from the unspiritual, deliberate raising of hands which is often the habit within some modern worship.

St. Paul, in his letter to the Philippians, Chapter 4, v. 6 says: "Have no anxiety about anything, but in everything by prayer and supplication let your requests be made known to God. And the peace of God, which passes all understanding, will keep (protect) your hearts and minds in Christ Jesus." We receive this peace in our heart as the Holy Spirit of God over-rules the turbulences and disquiets of our spirits. In so doing, our minds and emotions are quietened. Paul goes on to exhort us to feed our minds with wholesome things. When we do the opposite, or our minds are taken over by problems, disagreements or worry, we lose our peace. We end up in an "emotional state". That is because the thoughts that occupy our minds carry with them the spiritual force that is their nature - the point I made earlier.

A final note on which to end my thoughts on this subject. Have you noticed that the word "emotion" is not used in the Bible?

I will share one final insight or revelation that I believe was given to me by the Holy Spirit shortly before I completed this book.

It was in the context of events that happened to my wife Agnes at the time of the onset of her final illness. Throughout my life she had worked alongside me diligently in our business and latterly had shared in my Christian ministry. She had continued in all this despite the heart condition she had suffered from the age of forty. In all, she underwent three operations, two of which had involved open heart surgery. The last one, in February 1988, was to implant a porcine tissue valve, a replacement for the human mitral valve implanted two years earlier and which had unfortunately failed. This last operation was a great success. Then quite suddenly in February 1996 Agnes contracted a severe bacterial blood infection. Because of her chronic cardiac problem the infection attacked the mitral valve, creating a life-threatening condition. The job of killing off the bacteria took several weeks, during which time she received continuous intravenous doses of a very powerful antibiotic drug. It soon became evident that her illness, coupled with the delirium and toxaemia experienced during this period, was to have serious consequences. Her memory, already failing somewhat before her admission to hospital, was found to be severely impaired. Many months later it was discovered that her brain had been damaged by poisons from the infected valve, and later this condition was destined to worsen.

However, after leaving hospital, Agnes made a good recovery physically. Yet she was in a very weak and frightened state. Because of the damage to her short-term memory she was unable to judge properly the passage of time. She would experience panic attacks and feelings of desolation and loneliness, even when I was present in the house. A sense of fear of what might happen to her was an ever-present factor.

I recognised that all of these conditions could be considered spiritual. After all, fear, desolation, loneliness – I had met all these in my ministry to people over the years. I decided to pray about these things. I used authoritative prayers, as in deliverance. I also asked the Holy Spirit to fill her with God's love and peace, and to strengthen her spirit. A noticeable improvement took place. Then a new symptom appeared. Occasionally, particularly during the evening when she was inactive both physically and mentally, she would believe that I was not with her. She would in fact think that I was someone else. I found this very frightening. When on these occasions she eventually allowed me alongside, I would pray with her. Then she would quickly become her old self again. It may be possible to explain these events psychologically by the fact that, when in hospital, my regular twice-daily visits had seemed many days apart and that she had been reliving those traumatic times.

I decided to ask God how to pray. Almost immediately I found myself remembering something my pastor friend Bill had told me years before. Perhaps you will remember it - it concerned one of Satan's methods - one that I said you might find incredible! It was how, in times of weakness of spirit, soul and body, Satan would send in his demons in an attempt to destroy us. I prayed hard about this. One night a few days later I awoke to find in my mind the words: "Beware of marauding spirits!" Immediately I recalled that Scripture tells us to be watchful. We read: "Your adversary the Devil prowls around like a roaring lion, seeking someone to devour. Resist him, firm in your faith". (1 Peter 5, v 8, 9). I began to pray against marauding spirits. Then, two days later, in a time of shallow sleep I heard in my mind the words: "Pray against usurping spirits". I would never have thought up such words on my own. I knew they were from God. I looked up the word "usurp" in the dictionary, in order to remind myself of its exact meaning. It said: "To take possession of without right: intrusion." I shared all this with my vicar, and we prayed about it together. I also prayed with Agnes on the following day, finally taking authority over marauding and usurping spirits, binding their power and denying their right to harm her. The activity ceased forthwith! What might have seemed to the average person to have been a quite "over the top" approach had proved in fact to have been the right one.

As I have stated many times previously, the enemy does not give up easily. Only shortly after the above-mentioned events, Agnes started to talk a great deal about her father, who had died twenty-five years before. Then she thought she could sense that he was around, and to think that he might call to see her. I remembered that before he died her father had suffered for thirteen years from prostate cancer. During that period he had contacted the then well-known - and to Christians notorious - spiritualist healer, Harry Edwards, in an attempt to receive healing. He had also attended spiritualist meetings with the same purpose in mind. Though brought up in a Christian family, he had died without a true knowledge of Christ. A letter he had left for his children had revealed that he was spiritually most confused. I decided to refer again to a book I have read several times, "Healing the Family Tree", by Dr. Kenneth McAll (Sheldon Press, SPCK, London), in which he writes about souls that are not at rest. Particularly he writes about aborted babies and miscarriages. In my own ministry I have had, on occasions, needed to break soul-ties between dead people and the living, in the context of unconfessed sin which has held them in torment. All this is foreign territory to many Christians and is doctrinally unacceptable to some!

Agnes agreed to let me pray with her about her problem. What we did was straightforward. Having brought the matter before the Lord, we confessed the sins of her father and repented of them on his behalf. We claimed the forgiveness and cleansing offered to us through the shedding of the blood of Jesus Christ. I broke the curse put on him by his involvement with the occult and cut the soul-tie between Agnes and her father. We then gave his soul to God. From that time on there was no repetition of those unusual experiences, and Agnes found a new peace.

Doctors explain all the symptoms already described as being the result of old age and advancing senility. Certainly damage to the brain due to shortage of oxygen or to poisons in the bloodstream impair the memory and the ability to think clearly. Medicine has no answer to such damage, which is considered irreversible. Drugs are available for sedation and for the relief of symptoms. Yet I believe that we must not discount entirely the spiritual dimension in all of this. The truth is that we are spirit, soul and body, and their functions are interrelated. Medicine has special words to define every condition, whether "emotional", mental or physical. Even if it knows immediate causes, it cannot explain why there is a force or power to create such disease or condition, or where it comes from. So, for example, schizophrenia is described by its symptoms, and various other conditions as "syndromes", with a name given to them. What is a syndrome? By definition, merely a set of associated symptoms. We know that things like arthritis and a host of systemic illnesses can be caused by hormonal imbalance or chemical malfunction in the body. We now know more than at any time previously the role of genetic factors in illnesses such as cystic fibrosis. What is not understood is the power or mind behind such things, particularly the mind behind the creation of new and resistant strains of virus that can nullify the effects of hitherto potent drugs.

Of one thing I am certain. When the mind and power of God is brought to bear on our condition, whatever that may be, it restores to us a degree of the perfection that we see in Jesus Christ.

In the end, what we seek to do for others is to bring about in them such change that they conform as much as possible to God's original pattern for us. To this end, the Holy Spirit seeks to cleanse the human spirit and mind from all that is evil and unwholesome. The peace and pure life which then ensues brings health to soul and body also. Our soul life (self-life) reflects exactly the condition of our spirit. The countless emotions experienced in our soul reflect the whole spectrum of our desires, feelings and affections - wholesome or unwholesome. A way in which we can aid the Spirit in this work is through self-deliverance, as found in Romans Ch.6, mentioned earlier. Here Paul reminds us that the "self-life", with its carnal desires, must be destroyed through identification with Christ in his death. Then no longer would we be slaves to sin, but slaves to righteousness. This sanctification (being set apart for God in purity of life) can only be received by faith, just as at conversion we received Christ as our Saviour. Christians who counsel others and minister to them must set out to make this change real in their lives. Effecting deliverance alone, without any commitment to a new way of life, leaves the way open to the forces responsible for their original condition.

187

Ultimately, charismatic equipment lies at the heart of all we do. We must constantly remember that God's way does not lie in "understanding" what is happening in a client and in seeking to effect this by various techniques. It depends on "revelation" from the Holy Spirit who, working with us, shows us the spiritual needs of the person. Then together we can bring the power, love and mind of God to bear on the problem. The emotional state of those whom we help will tell us something about the condition of their spirit. We will be able to discern progress and know when healing of the spirit has been achieved. If those we help become committed to living a pure life in the Holy Spirit, they will thereafter experience a gradual strengthening of their own spirit. They will know deliverance from the "up-and-down" emotional experiences found in the life of the still carnal Christian.

I realise that what I have written in this book is subjective. As a result it may not all be taken on board or believed. The insights I have shared in this last chapter are subjective also. I also recognise that, even if true, they represent only a tiny fraction of the spiritual revelation that God longs to give us as fellow-workers with Christ in his Church. I ask you earnestly to seek for yourself more and more of that revelation. Then you will continue to increase in God's love, power and truth, as the Holy Spirit leads you to minister to others.

ISBN 1-41204495-2